The Tapestry of God

Spiritual Mobilization and Vision Alignment

Apostle Patrick K Nepay

Foreword by

Bishop Darlingston Johnson

Praise for THE TAPESTRY OF GOD: SPIRITUAL MOBILIZATION & VISION ALIGNMENT

"In his book, The Tapestry of God, Apostle Patrick K. Nepay offers a profound, Spirit-filled revelation of how God weaves the lives of believers into His eternal design through divine purpose, vision alignment, and spiritual mobilization. Drawing from decades of ministry experience, rich biblical insight, and personal encounters with God, he reveals that every believer is a thread intentionally placed by the Master Weaver. Wherever you are and however you serve, your life is not insignificant. You are a vital part of God's divine tapestry. Your journey and obedience are being woven together to reveal His glory. This compelling work will inspire you to embrace your place in God's grand scheme, design and walk boldly in your divine purpose."
~Bishop S. Musa Korfeh, Assistant Presiding Bishop, HIMU; Diocesan Bishop – North & South America, Europe, Australia & Asia, Senior Pastor, Harvest Houston

"The Tapestry of God is a profound and timely revelation that brings clarity to life's most difficult moments. With rich biblical insight and powerful imagery, it reminds us that what appears chaotic and broken is, in fact, being masterfully woven by the hand of God. This book anchors the soul in hope and calls every reader to see their life through Heaven's eternal perspective. It is both deeply comforting and boldly empowering."
~Michael L. Mathews, VP for Global Learning and Innovation, Oral Roberts University

"The Tapestry of God is an inspirational work that reflects both the call of God and the pattern of Jesus Christ. It carries a message that encourages believers to understand God's purpose and design for their lives. I am happy to endorse this book."
~Apostle Napoleon Blamon, Senior Pastor, Harvest Intercontinental Church Trenton and Philadelphia; Harvest Intercontinental Church Philadelphia

"I have known the author for more than three decades and have witnessed firsthand how God has processed, transformed, and elevated him into the man he is today. Because of this journey, I understand why he is uniquely positioned to write *The Tapestry of God: Spiritual Mobilization and Vision Alignment*. I strongly recommend this book to believers of every level. It captures the true reality of who God has made us to be and how He intentionally shapes us into what we were meant to become. Holding this book in your hands means you have made the right choice and by the time you finish reading, you will not be the same. Bravo, and God bless you!"
~Bishop Dr. Apostle M. Wolo Belleh Diocesan Bishop & Dean Harvest Intercontinental Ministries Unlimited, First Diocese / Harvest Intercontinental Cathedral

"The Tapestry of God is a theologically rich and spiritually incisive work that brings clarity to the intentional design of God in the life of every believer. Apostle Patrick K. Nepay masterfully articulates how divine purpose, process, and destiny are woven together by the hand of God. Its themes—particularly the profound illumination of Psalm 23—have already demonstrated transformative impact within ministry settings where they have been taught. This book is a timely and essential resource for leaders and believers seeking to walk confidently in God's sovereign plan."
~Bishop Apostle Davidetta G. Tarnue Presiding Bishop, Gates Agape Ministries International

"Apostle Patrick Nepay delivers a divine mandate in *The Tapestry of God*. With prophetic clarity and apostolic depth, he reveals how God weaves lives, destinies, ministries, and visions into one unified purpose. This book will not only challenge you—it will align you, mobilize you, and ignite you for Kingdom impact. A must-read for every serious believer and leader."
~Rev. Joe Nimely, Assistant Pastor Harvest Intercontinental Church–Baltimore; National Secretary, Harvest Intercontinental Ministries Unlimited – US District

This book is dedicated to the remembrance and honoring of my beloved parents, **Mr. Nicholas Nepay** and **Mrs. Elizabeth Koffa Nepay**, whose faith, resilience, and devotion to God laid the foundation of my life and calling. Their prayers continue to speak, and their legacy still guides every step I take.

To **Sister Rose Gabriel** (**née** Gadegbeku), a pioneering Liberian nun whose compassion and sacrifice changed the trajectory of my life. After my father's passing when I was just ten years old, a year and a half later, you became God's instrument of promise, sponsoring my education and opening the door that led me to St. Mary's Elementary and St. Patrick's High Schools. Your kindness endures in each life touched through my ministry.

To **Rev. Russ Tatro**, Founder of Living Word Ministries and the Monrovia Bible Training Center, whose mentorship awakened my calling to the mission field. Under your guidance, I heard and accepted the divine summons that has formed my life's work. Your obedience to God served as the catalyst for my own.

To my beloved wife, **Dr. Kona Facia Freeman Nepay**, whose steadfast love, wisdom, and partnership strengthen my hands for the work of ministry. You walk beside me with grace, honor, and distinction. Your support is a divine gift, and your presence is a blessing beyond measure.

May this work stand as evidence of the God who weaves every life into His eternal tapestry.

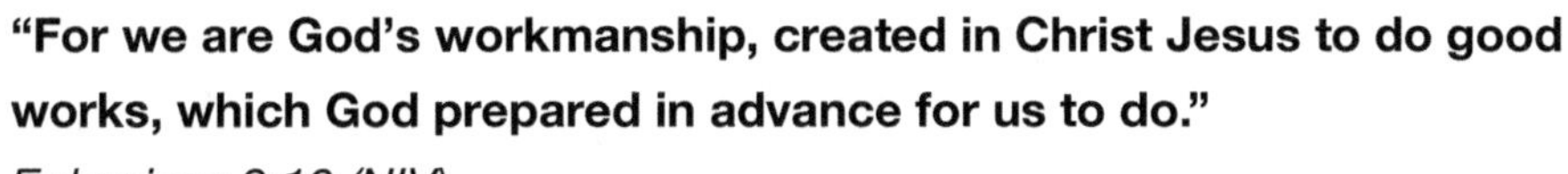

"For we are God's workmanship, created in Christ Jesus to do good works, which God prepared in advance for us to do."
Ephesians 2:10 (NIV)

The Tapestry of God

Spiritual Mobilization and Vision Alignment

Apostle Patrick K Nepay

Foreword by

Bishop Darlingston Johnson

FOREWORD

In every generation, God raises voices to shift our focus from earthly limitations to heaven's perspective. The Tapestry of God: Spiritual Mobilization and Vision Alignment is one such voice—an invitation to see, trust, and align with His divine work.

At the heart of this book, Rev. Patrick Nepay, calls us to adopt the "weaver's perspective." While we often view life from beneath the loom—seeing only knots, tangles, and disjointed threads—God works from above with precision and love. What appears chaotic from below is intentional from above; our struggles are not wasted threads but chosen ones, woven into a purpose far greater than we can comprehend.

The strength of this message rests on three pillars:

•Hope: A resilient confidence in God's nature that anchors the soul when life pulls tight.

•Identity: The realization that you are God's intentional workmanship, crafted with specific gifts and experiences.

•Grace: The "golden thread" and sustaining force that weaves human weakness into divine strength.

Grounding these truths in Scripture, Rev. Nepay explores the lives of Joseph, Moses, and Esther to show that delays and wilderness seasons are often divine positioning. These narratives prove a consistent truth: God is always weaving.

The Tapestry of God is both theological and practical, moving readers from passive observation to active participation in God's vision. It challenges you to embrace your process and recognize that nothing is insignificant in the hands of the Master Weaver.

In a time of searching, this work offers an enduring perspective that anchors the soul and fuels purpose. As you read, may you find peace in the process and trust the Weaver more deeply, knowing your life is beautifully and eternally woven into His masterpiece.

Your thread matters.

Bishop Darlingston G. Johnson is the Presiding Bishop of Harvest Intercontinental Ministries Unlimited

Preface

"For we are His workmanship, created in Christ Jesus for good works, which God prepared beforehand that we should walk in them."
- Ephesians 2:10

As we embark on this spiritual journey, we invite you to join us in reflecting on the beautiful truth that God is weaving our lives into His divine masterpiece. Just as a Master Weaver threads each strand into a beautiful tapestry, the Father is working all things together for our good and His glory (Romans 8:28).

In this book, we will explore three foundational truths that will anchor us in our faith:

1. Our hope in Christ is the anchor of our souls, firm and secure (Hebrews 6:19). This hope keeps us steady on the loom of God's eternal purpose, even when life pulls and stretches us.

2. We are God's workmanship, His carefully crafted threads, designed for good works (Ephesians 2:10). Each of us is uniquely threaded, fashioned, colored, and textured, destined to fit perfectly into the role we are to play and the pattern of His Kingdom we are designed for.

3. It is God's grace that secures us (1 Corinthians 15:10). Grace is the shuttle that moves us across the loom, ensuring our lives are interwoven with divine strength, not

human striving.

May you be encouraged to trust the Weaver's work in your life as you journey through these pages. Every trial, every stretching, and every knot of pressure is a spiritual awakening, securing you for His glory. May God mobilize, form, and expand us as partners in building His church and expanding the Father's Kingdom, reflecting the beauty of His divine tapestry.

My journey with the Lord began long before I understood the language of calling. The earliest seeds of my spiritual formation were planted through the life of my biological father, Mr. Nicholas Nepay. He was a devoted believer—loving, caring, and a faithful provider whose prayer life and unwavering devotion to God shaped the spiritual atmosphere of our home. Though my time with him was short, his example left a deep imprint on my heart.

I was only nine years old when my father passed away. Losing such a godly and nurturing father at a tender age felt like being robbed of the greatest gift God had given me. The grief created a silent distance between me and God, and for nearly a year I refused to step into a church. Yet even in that season of quiet rebellion, I found myself imitating my father's devotion—as if maintaining his spiritual legacy could fill the void he left behind.

It was during this time that the Lord spoke clearly to my heart: **"I will be a Father to you."** From that moment, I sensed His presence in a way that convinced me that divine purpose rested upon my life.

After being out of school for two years, my late brother

Nicholas—named after our father—told me that a woman named Sister Rose Gabriel, a Catholic nun who once taught me at Cathedral School, had been asking about me. Sister Rose Gabriel (née Gadegbeku) was one of the first Liberian nuns ordained in 1969 under the Order of Bernardine Sisters of the Roman Catholic Church. She insisted that I come to her immediately. She took hold of my education, ensured I returned to school, and guided me all the way to St. Patrick's High School. When she suddenly passed away in a tragic accident, I felt abandoned once again. Yet divine favor began to follow me in ways I could not explain.

In 1979, after a fierce spiritual encounter in a dream, I surrendered my life to Jesus Christ as my Lord and Savior. My cousin later told me he had fallen off the bed while I wrestled and spoke words he could not understand. That encounter marked the beginning of my spiritual awakening.

In 1989, God arranged my path to the mission field through my mentor, the late Reverend Russ Tatro. During my final year of Bible school, a signup sheet for the mission field sat untouched for weeks. Wanting to encourage others, I placed my name on the list, planning to remove it on the last day. But God had other plans. The list was collected early, and my name was the only one on it. What began as a harmless attempt to motivate others became God's humorous and unmistakable call on my life. The mission field became a place of spiritual warfare and divine protection. I faced battles that tested my faith, survived the outbreak of the civil crisis, and witnessed God hide my life in the very place where the war began. My journey since then has been a tapestry of supernatural encounters—each one a chapter worthy of its own book.

Up close, the struggles, the waiting, the setbacks, and the knots of pressure in our lives can seem like chaos. They can appear meaningless, random, or even destructive. This book is dedicated to revealing a profound, stabilizing truth: your life is not a random spool of yarn, but a specifically chosen thread being expertly guided by a sovereign, loving hand.

For example, Abraham's life is a profound representation of a Godgiven purpose brought to fulfillment. God established his purpose long before its manifestation: he was called to be the **father of many nations** and a **source of blessing to all the families of the earth** (Genesis 12:1–3). Yet Abraham was childless, advanced in age, and facing biological impossibilities. His purpose required supernatural intervention. His journey unfolded through a series of divine encounters—covenants, promises, and reaffirmations. Despite delays and human limitations, Abraham *"hoped against hope"* (Romans 4:18), trusting that the God who called him was also the God who would fulfill the promise. When his son Isaac was finally born, it became clear that purpose is not achieved by human strength but by divine orchestration.

Abraham's transformation—from Abram to Abraham—reveals that God not only gives purpose but also shapes identity to match that purpose. His life demonstrates that when God establishes a purpose, He also provides the endurance, faith, and divine timing necessary to bring it to pass.

Over the coming chapters, drawing foundational truth from Ephesians 2:10, Hebrews 6:19, and 1 Corinthians 15:10, we will explore three foundational spiritual realities that define our existence on the Loom. And what is a Loom? According to Merriam-Webster, a loom is a device used to weave threads or yarn to produce cloth. The chief purpose of a loom is to hold the "warp threads" under tension to enable the interweaving of the "weft threads." Therefore, the Heavenly Loom is God's unshakable sovereignty. The threads are our lives, fragile yet spiritually formidable, unfathomably unique, strategically positioned, and divinely chosen. The design is God's eternal glory revealed in Jesus through His church.

The Unshakable Hope (Hebrews 6:19):

This hope is the anchor of your soul, firm and secure. It is the assurance that keeps your thread taut, steadying you on the Loom even when life attempts to pull and stretch you thin.

Consider the life of Joseph. If you looked at the "yarn" of his early years, you would see nothing but tangles: the jagged tear of betrayal by his brothers, the dark stains of false accusation, and the long, dusty years of waiting in an Egyptian prison. To Joseph, sitting in a cell for a crime he didn't commit, the thread likely felt frayed and meaningless. Yet, the "sovereign, loving hand" was never still. Every setback was a setup. The knots of his suffering were the very grip God used to pull him into the palace of Pharaoh. Joseph was elevated to second-in-command of Egypt, not for his own status, but for a global rescue mission. During a massive famine, Joseph was positioned to save the entire region—including the very family that betrayed him—from starvation. His life culminates in the profound realization found in Genesis 50:20: "You intended to harm me, but God intended it for good to accomplish what is now being done, the saving of many lives." What Joseph once saw as a chaotic spool of misfortune was a masterfully woven tapestry of salvation.

The Divine Workmanship (Ephesians 2:10):

You are his handiwork. You are his carefully crafted work, his masterpiece. You are uniquely fashioned, colored, and textured. Your calling, gifts, and even your pains are the perfect elements destined to fit precisely into the role God designed for you within His Kingdom pattern. Science itself affirms this divine intentionality. According to the Federal Bureau of Investigation, no two fingerprints have ever been found to be identical, even among identical twins, whose nearly identical DNA still produces distinct ridge patterns. Embryological studies show that fingerprints form through unique pressures and movements in the womb, ensuring that every human being carries a pattern that has never existed before. Although we are all made from the same basic elements, God intentionally differentiated each of us. You are a living example of His divine workmanship. A vivid biblical example of this securing grace is seen in the life of Paul. He confessed, *"But by the grace of God I am what I am… I labored more abundantly than they all, yet not I, but the grace of God which was with me"* (1 Corinthians 15:10). Paul's strength, identity, and effectiveness were not the result of human striving but the outworking of divine grace. Grace held him, carried him, empowered him, and secured every assignment God placed on his life. This same grace is the golden thread that stabilizes your journey across the Loom of God.

The Unfolding Vision

Through the potent, prophetic threads of Jacob, Joseph and Moses, we will see how personal destiny is always tied to a corporate, kingdom-sized vision. Their stories prove that the pits, the betrayals, the exiles, and the wrestling are not roadblocks, but the very mechanism by which the Master Weaver prepares, secures, and exalts His chosen threads. What the enemy intends for evil, God always reweaves for good (Genesis 50:20). Have you experienced a pivot in your life that while at first seemed unreasonable or inconvenient, eventually revealed itself to be something that saved you? Have you ever looked at yourself in the mirror after a catastrophic life storm and thought: "Oh, that's why." God uses these storms to renew us, to revive us, and to call us to remember his grace and intentionality upon our lives. Grace is the gold thread that secures every strand. Grace is the power that moves you across the Loom, ensuring your life is interwoven with divine strength, not human striving. As you start this period of reading and reflection, may the Holy Spirit, the Master Weaver, open your eyes. May you come to recognize that the back of the tapestry you often see in your own life, full of knots, tangles, and what feels like confusion, is already being transformed into the brilliant, beautiful face of a masterpiece in the making. Every thread is placed with intention. Every color has purpose. Every tension has meaning. All of it is designed for the eternal glory of Christ. Trust the Weaver. Your life is intentional.

This book is a call to Spiritual Mobilization—a summons for believers everywhere to align their lives with God's eternal purpose for His Church in this critical hour. It invites you to move from living as an isolated thread to becoming an intentional, Spiritwoven part of a global tapestry of revival, unity, and Kingdom expansion. What began as a focused journey within one community now extends to the wider Body of Christ, offering a prophetic invitation to participate in God's worldwide apostolic movement—one committed to planting churches, equipping believers, and advancing the Kingdom across nations. Just as a master weaver skillfully places every strand, the Father is weaving our lives, our callings, and our collective mission into His unfolding masterpiece.

> Hebrews 6:19 reminds us that **hope in Christ is the anchor of our souls**, firm and secure. This hope keeps us steady on the loom of God's eternal purpose, even when life pulls and stretches us.
>
> Ephesians 2:10 (NIV) declares: "For we are God's handiwork, created in Christ Jesus to do good works, which God prepared in advance for us to do." Believers are His carefully crafted threads, designed for good works. Each of us is uniquely threaded, fashioned, colored, and textured, destined to fit perfectly into the role we are to play and the pattern of His Kingdom we are designed for.
>
> 1 Corinthians 15:10 reveals that **it is grace that secures us**. Paul testifies: *"By the grace of God I am what I am."* Grace is the shuttle that moves us across the loom, ensuring our lives are interwoven with divine strength, not human striving.

I have seen the Weaver's hand most clearly when the threads of my life seemed most frayed by the enemy. Early in my ministry, I was assigned to Yekepa, Nimba County, in Liberia. Before relocating, I went to "spy out" the land, unaware that the spiritual territory was already claiming ownership.

On my final night there, a woman appeared in my dream, her hair standing stiff and wild on all sides. She was filled with a territorial rage, accusing me of trying to destroy her life. She lunged at my chest with a sharp object, and I woke up so abruptly I had rolled across the bed.

Later, after moving to Yekepa, I found myself praying in a church until the pitch-black hours of the evening. As I walked out into the tall weeds, I heard the unmistakable, chilling hiss of a snake in the dark. I couldn't see it, but I could hear it moving. In that moment, the three truths of the loom became reality:

- **The Anchor:** My hope wasn't in my sight, but in the God who held my soul steady.
- **The Workmanship:** I knew I wasn't in that field by accident; I was a thread strategically placed for a Kingdom pattern.
- **The Shuttle of Grace:** A supernatural calm took over. I refused to run. I walked forward in the dark, confident that the Weaver was moving me exactly where I needed to be.

It was only after I reached the light that human fear tried to overtake me. But the Spirit whispered a reminder: **Jehovah is covering my life and destiny.** My life was not being unraveled by the serpent; it was being tightly woven into God's sovereign design.

Reflection Questions

- Where in your life do you feel "pulled and stretched" right now?

- Can you see that tension not as a breaking point, but as the Weaver tightening the fabric of your character?

We recognize that we are not isolated threads left to decay, be easily broken, and forgotten. We are part of something larger, eternal, and beautiful, woven in the tapestry of God. Though we may not yet see the full design, we trust the Weaver's work. Every trial, every stretching, and every knot of pressure is a spiritual awakening, securing us for His glory.

Chapter 1

The Call of God

1 Peter 2:9

9 But you are a chosen generation, a royal priesthood, a holy nation, His own special people, that you may proclaim the praises of Him who called you out of darkness into His marvelous light;

Hebrews 6:19

19 This hope we have as an anchor of the soul, both sure and steadfast, and which enters the Presence behind the veil,

Ephesians 2:10

10 For we are His workmanship, created in Christ Jesus for good works, which God prepared beforehand that we should walk in them.

1 Corinthians 15:10

10 But by the grace of God I am what I am, and His grace toward me was not in vain; but I labored more abundantly than they all, yet not I, but the grace of God which was with me.

A loom is a device used to weave threads of fabric into a tapestry. The chief purpose of a loom is to hold the "warp threads" under tension to enable the interweaving of the "weft threads."

In weaving, warp and weft are two sets of threads that are interlaced to create fabric. The "warp" threads run vertically from top to bottom on the loom and form the structure of the fabric. These are the strong, vertical threads that are held under tension on a loom. They provide the basic structure and strength of the fabric. They are the backbone of a cloth. These threads reveal the heavenly connection and support that Heaven has with believers on the earth. The weft is comprised of threads that run horizontally and are woven through the warp threads to create the fabric's surface and pattern. These horizontal threads are woven at the top and bottom of the warp threads to make the pattern and provide the texture and strength of the fabric. The weft adds color, beauty, design, and richness to the fabric. A loom is the frame on which threads are arranged and woven into cloth. It is the foundation where patterns are determined through vision and securely structured. Spiritually, a heavenly loom represents the divine framework of God's eternal purpose, where every life is placed, measured, and woven according to His sovereign plan.

A tapestry is a woven masterpiece in a textile that displays beauty, depth, and meaning when viewed as a whole. Up close, in the natural setting, the threads may appear disconnected, uneven, or uncertain. But from heaven's perspective, the Divine Tapestry reveals God's story of redemption, interweaving generations, nations, and individuals into a majestic display of His love, beauty, and glory.

Threads are the fibers of a fabric. They are not chosen at random. The Weaver fashions each strand based on color (the blood and power of the Cross of Christ), texture (the value and beauty in Christ), and strength or weakness (endurance), for its role in Christ's design. God sovereignly calls believers before the foundation of the world, places them in harmony with others, and secures them through trials and knots of grace. The thread begins with the person, unique and fearfully made. It then becomes a vessel of honor shaped by the loom. It takes form as a mantle, representing calling and covering. Finally, it is covered in Grace, the golden thread that runs through every crack of a believer's life, empowering them to shine beyond natural beauty and capacity.

Hope anchors a believer in Christ (Hebrews 6:19). **Purpose defines a believer's life** (Ephesians 2:10). A mantle feels heavy, but it covers, elevates, and empowers a believer in authority. **Grace then shapes a believer in destiny** (1 Corinthians 15:10). What may look like a broken strand in a believer's life is usually the Master Weaver's knitting of eternal glory in the making.

To be woven by a Heavenly Loom in a Divine Tapestry means that your life is not unintentional. Your story may appear conflicting. Your frame may look weak on the outside, but inside, there is a hidden glory. Your struggles are part of God's strategic plan in redemption. They are all part of an eternal masterpiece of healing, deliverance, redemption, and beauty, working together in divine harmony. You are a chosen thread (1 Peter 2:9) in a royal design, fitted in a divine alignment with others in Christ, stretched by trials, clothed by anointing, secured by grace, and displayed in the glory of Christ. The Holy Spirit is not an abstract force, but the living, active presence of God, carefully woven in detail, into the lives of believers. He is the divine tapestry of power, guidance, and transformation. The Holy Spirit's work is not a relic of the past but a vibrant, unfolding masterpiece. Believers should embrace His manifestations with expectancy, testing all things (1 Thessalonians 5:21) while pursuing the fullness of His presence.

"For the tapestry of the Spirit is still being woven, thread by thread, life by life, until the day we see face to face." (1

Corinthians 13:12).

Meditation:

Let Hebrews 6:19 guide your thoughts as you consider how your life is being woven by divine intent and how every thread, joy, pain, success, and patience, is part of His perfect design. When was the last time you laughed out loud? It was by design. When was the last time you cried inconsolably? It was by design. As were both your successes and failures. It is difficult to hear this. But if we are to praise him for our seasons of abundance, we are to also find intention during our seasons of lack. God's handiwork is perfect.

Chapter 2

The Journey of Faith

Genesis 50:20: Hebrews 6:19; Romans 8:28

Joseph's life is one of the most compelling narratives in Scripture. Born to Jacob and Rachel, Joseph was the favored son, marked by a richly ornamented coat that symbolized his father, Jacob's, love and his unique destiny. At a young age, Joseph received dreams from God, foretelling his rise to prominence. These dreams, however, stirred jealousy among his brothers, who sold him into slavery and deceived their father into believing he was dead. When his enslavement led him to Egypt, Joseph's life seemed to unravel further. As a slave in Potiphar's house, he rose to a position of trust, only to be falsely accused by Potiphar's wife and thrown into prison. Even in the depths of confinement, Joseph's faith and integrity shone. He interpreted dreams for Pharaoh's officials, a gift that eventually brought him before Pharaoh himself. In a single day, Joseph was elevated from prisoner to prime minister, entrusted with the task of saving Egypt and surrounding nations from a devastating famine.

Through years of betrayal, slavery, and imprisonment, Joseph's life was being woven into God's greater plan. His trials were not wasted; they were the knots that secured him to his divine purpose. When famine struck, Joseph's wisdom and leadership not only preserved Egypt but also reunited him with his family. In a moment of profound forgiveness, Joseph declared to his brothers, *"You meant evil against me, but God meant it for good, to bring it about that many people should be kept alive"* (Genesis 50:20).

Joseph's story is a prophetic thread in God's tapestry, illustrating how trials refine and position believers for their divine calling. His life points to Christ, who was also rejected, betrayed, and humbled, yet exalted to bring salvation to many.

Joseph's life was woven into God's covenant for Israel, and by the Spirit, it becomes a model of how God weaves believers and the Church into His eternal tapestry in Christ. Joseph, as any faithful believer, was chosen, stretched, tested, and exalted. Like Joseph, believers are chosen and destined before birth (Jeremiah 1:5; Ephesians 1:4). Believers are often stretched by trials that feel like betrayal, slavery, or prison. They are grace-secured until God brings them into the place of fruitfulness.

"By the grace of God I am what I am…" (1 Corinthians 15:10).

The thread that Joseph's life was woven in and the pattern it had to follow in God's tapestry was not about or for himself. Israel's preservation was the result of God's intentional and unwavering commitment to His covenant people. Through seasons of famine, threat, and uncertainty, the Lord was quietly securing the lineage through which His promises would unfold. What appeared fragile in the natural was, in truth, held firmly by His sovereign hand. Every challenge became a thread He wove into their story—threads of protection, continuity, and divine purpose—ensuring that His redemptive plan for the nations would remain intact. Likewise, the believer's life is woven not only for their personal destiny, but also for the Body of Christ. The Church is God's corporate tapestry where every believer is a thread (1 Corinthians 12:12–14). As Joseph was fitted into Israel's covenantal future, so too are believers fitted into the Church's future for Kingdom expansion. Like Joseph, the believers must be aligned with God's vision and mission for the Church.

> *"From whom the whole body, joined and knit together by what every joint supplies…" (Ephesians 4:16).*

The Holy Spirit spun Joseph's life together with dreams, trials, and favor into the pattern with His plan for Israel. For believers and the Church, the Spirit weaves them into a corporate thread. As a believer is sanctified, refined, and spiritually empowered and sustained through their union with Christ and His Church, so too the Church is to prosper and be financially empowered and sustained through the wealth of believers. The Spirit weaves us together as one body, making us a vessel for revival, unity, and global mission. When Joseph became successful, he sent for "Israel" (Jacob) and his sons. When the Church was delivered from bondage, Joseph's bones, along with his posterity, were delivered also. Believers cannot expect to withhold their resources from the Body of Christ and look to the head of the body for healing, deliverance, and divine favor.

> *"…you also, like living stones, are being built into a spiritual house…" (1 Peter 2:5).*

Joseph's thread points to Christ, rejected, betrayed, humbled, yet exalted to save many. The Church is now woven into Christ's redemptive tapestry: believers are strands of His mission. The body is the display of His wisdom and glory to the nations (Ephesians 3:10). Just as Joseph's suffering saved Israel, the church's witness, sacrifice, and faith preserve believers and nations in Christ. What God weaves together cannot be undone

(Ecclesiastes 3:14). Joseph's life proves that trials and hardships do not undo God's plan; they secure it. For believers and the Church, their knots (tests, persecutions, pressures) are not wasted; they hold them firmly in His tapestry. Hardships do not stop believers' commitment to the Body of Christ. Their hope is anchored together in Jesus (Hebrews 6:19). Together, their destiny is secure, because grace holds them together in unity.

> *"It is a faithful saying: For if we be dead with Him, we shall also rise with Him, we shall also live with Him: If we suffer, we shall also reign with Him: If we deny Him, He also will deny us (2 Timothy 2:11-12).*

> *"Then the Lord said to Abram, 'Know for certain that your descendants will be strangers in a country not their own, and they will be enslaved and mistreated four hundred years. But I will punish the nation they serves as slaves, and afterward they will come out with great possessions.'" (Genesis 15:13–14)*

In this prophetic declaration, God laid the loom of covenant blessing. The "loom" here is God's unchangeable decree, an unshakable frame on which the destiny of Israel would be woven. Every thread in the life of Israel had to be aligned with this prophetic word. Egypt would become both a place of bondage and birthing, a place of refining in which Israel would transform from a family into a nation. This covenant word set the pattern of the tapestry, and Joseph's life became one of the first threads woven into its fulfillment. Long before Joseph's birth, his life was prophesied in God's word to Abraham. Through him, Israel entered Egypt, not by accident, but by prophetic necessity. Thus, Joseph's thread teaches us: **Before we were formed, we were known, chosen, and fitted**

into God's eternal tapestry for His glory and the purpose of His kingdom.

***

Joseph's story cannot be fully understood without considering the life of his father, Jacob, a central figure in God's covenant with Israel. Jacob, later renamed Israel, was the son of Isaac and the grandson of Abraham, through whom God established His covenant to bless all nations. Jacob's life was marked by struggle and transformation, a journey that shaped not only his destiny but also the destiny of his descendants.

From birth, Jacob's life was intertwined with conflict. He was born grasping the heel of his twin brother, Esau, a foreshadowing of the rivalry that would define much of his early years. True to his name, which means "supplanter" or "heel-grabber," Jacob cunningly secured both the birthright and the blessing that traditionally belonged to Esau. This deception led to years of estrangement from his family, as Jacob fled to his uncle Laban's household to escape Esau's wrath.

In Laban's house, Jacob experienced both blessing and hardship. He fell in love with Rachel, Joseph's mother, but was deceived into marrying her sister, Leah, first. After years of labor, Jacob finally married Rachel, the woman he loved, and she bore him Joseph after a long period of barrenness. Jacob's deep affection for Rachel made Joseph the favored son, a status that would later provoke jealousy among Joseph's brothers.

Jacob's life was also marked by encounters with God that transformed him. At Bethel, he dreamed of a ladder reaching to heaven, a vision of God's covenant promises. Years later, he wrestled with God at Peniel, where he was renamed Israel, meaning "he struggles with God." This moment symbolized Jacob's transformation from a man who relied on his own cunning to one who depended on God's grace.

As a father, Jacob's favoritism toward Joseph created tension within his family. Yet, his love for Joseph was rooted in the deep bond he shared with Rachel. When Joseph was presumed dead, Jacob was inconsolable, believing he had lost the son of his old age and the living memory of his beloved Rachel. His grief endured for years until the miraculous reunion with Joseph in Egypt, a moment that reaffirmed God's faithfulness to His covenant promises.

Jacob's life, like Joseph's, was a thread in God's divine tapestry. His struggles, failures, and triumphs were all woven into the fulfillment of God's plan to establish a nation through his descendants. Jacob's story reminds us that God's purposes often unfold through imperfect people, and His covenant faithfulness endures through every trial and transformation.

Specifically chosen threads are custom-made for master weavers. Though the thread may appear small, unseen, weak, and sometimes unattractive and insignificant, once placed in the hands of a master weaver, His mastery makes it become a significant part of a delicate whole. A single thread by itself looks ordinary, fragile, and even useless. Yet, when guided by the hand of the Master Weaver, that thread becomes important to the beauty of a tapestry.

Joseph was chosen early and set apart, with dreams of greatness (Genesis 37:5–7). His dreams were not self-made but divinely woven into him before he understood them. Yet, being chosen does not exempt believers from trials. Instead, it attracts them. His brothers despised him, stripped him of his coat of divine tapestry, and sold him as a slave. To the natural eye, his thread was being cut off, but in God's loom, it was being stretched and fitted. Being chosen means being tested. The loom of God often stretches His chosen threads before displaying them. Joseph's thread was stretched by trials. In Jacob's house, he was gifted, but envied and thrown into a pit. In Potiphar's house, he was faithful but falsely accused and thrown in jail. In prison, he was forgotten after interpreting dreams. In abandonment, he was unseen for years, yet God's hand was silently weaving his destiny.

The knots of jealousy and betrayal, the friction of temptation, and the pressure of confinement did not destroy Joseph's thread, but rather, secured him. What seemed like setbacks were God's way of keeping Joseph's life aligned with his divine destiny. *"We have this hope as an anchor for the soul, firm and secure."* (Hebrews 6:19). Joseph's anchor was his trust in God, not his circumstances. Joseph's thread was revealed through God's pattern. At Pharaoh's summons, Joseph was lifted from the place of confinement to the place of dominion in a single day (Genesis 41:14). The dream God gave him as a boy was fulfilled in God's perfect timing. Looking back, Joseph saw his thread in the divine tapestry: *"You meant evil against me, but God meant it for good, to bring it about that many people should be kept alive."* (Genesis 50:20).

A believer may feel unseen or insignificant, but in God's loom, they are necessary. Their trials are not wasted; they are the knots that anchor them to His purpose. Their story, like Joseph's, will testify that what was meant for evil is woven for good (Romans 8:28). There is a Joseph's thread in every believer. Joseph's rise was not by human merit, but by God's grace weaving through every detail in his life: In the pit, grace set him up and escorted him to where he was to receive his purpose and fulfillment. In Potiphar's house, grace preserved him in integrity. In prison, grace gave him favor and prophetic interpretation. In Pharaoh's palace, grace exalted him to govern a nation. Paul echoes this when he says:

> *"By the grace of God I am what I am, and His grace toward me was not in vain." (1 Corinthians 15:10).*

Joseph's thread of divine weaving shows us that God takes what looks broken and fragile and weaves it into strength and beauty. Like Joseph, the believer's story may appear frayed in moments of betrayal, loss, or waiting, but in the end, it will testify: "God meant it for good."

Chapter 3

The Make-Up of a Divine Tapestry

Ephesians 4:1-6 (NKJV)

I, therefore, the prisoner [a]of the Lord, [b]beseech you to walk worthy of the calling with which you were called, 2) with all lowliness and gentleness, with longsuffering, bearing with one another in love, 3) endeavoring to keep the unity of the Spirit in the bond of peace. 4) There is one body and one Spirit, just as you were called in one hope of your calling; 5) one Lord, one faith, one baptism; 6) one God and Father of all, who is above all, and through all, and in you all.

The stories of Jacob and Joseph in scripture are not isolated tales of personal ethics and glory, but rather events in the greater scheme of God forming a covenant community for Himself.

An individual's spiritual destiny is tied to the corporate body. This is the principle set forth in Joseph's story. His dreams (Genesis 37:5-11) were not primarily about his personal success, but about the security of the house of Israel (the divine institution).

Joseph, the favored son of Jacob, was gifted by God with prophetic dreams of leadership, which fueled the jealousy of his brothers. This tension led to a dramatic series of trials and triumphs:

- Betrayal: His brothers sold him into slavery in Egypt, where he served in the house of Potiphar.
- False Accusation: Despite his integrity, he was wrongly imprisoned after being framed by Potiphar's wife.

- Divine Timing: In prison, Joseph interpreted the dreams of Pharaoh's cupbearer and baker, eventually leading him to interpret Pharaoh's own troubling dreams about a coming famine.
- Exaltation: Impressed by his wisdom, Pharaoh appointed Joseph as Vizier of Egypt, second only to the throne.
- Redemption: During the famine, Joseph's brothers came to Egypt for food. Instead of seeking revenge, Joseph provided for them, stating that what they meant for evil, God intended for good—ultimately saving the lineage of Israel.

His brothers' attempt to cut him off was, in their minds, a rejection of his God-given destiny and his connection to them. It was a spiritual attack, an attempt to spiritually separate him:

> *"Come now, let's kill him and throw him into one of these cisterns... Then we'll see what comes of his dreams." (Genesis 37:20).*

The divine result was that, instead of destruction, this act of separation became the very mechanism God used to save the family. Joseph later declares the divine perspective: *"You intended to harm me, but God intended it for good to accomplish what is now being done, the saving of many lives." (Genesis 50:20).* The "many lives" were the covenant family—the emerging nation of Israel. An individual believer's resources, gifts, calling, and destiny (Ephesians 2:10) are given by God through the Spirit for the building up and equipping of the Body of Christ, the New Covenant divine institution, not for personal possession and praise. 1 Corinthians 12:7, 12-14, 27 says, *"Now to each one the manifestation of the Spirit is given for the common good... Just as a body, though one, has many parts, but all its many parts from one body, so it is with Christ... You are the Body of Christ, and each one of you is a part of it."* A person with the gift of teaching is not meant to be a solo act but to equip the saints (Ephesians 4:11-12). To separate from the body is to rob the body of its function and to rob oneself of its covering and purpose, leading to spiritual ineffectiveness and vulnerability.

While Joseph was suffering, he was also being strategically positioned. Because he was in prison, he eventually met the Pharaoh's cupbearer, which led to him interpreting Pharaoh's dreams about an upcoming global famine. Because of this, Joseph was promoted to Vizier (second-in-command) of Egypt. He spent seven years storing up massive amounts of grain.

This is where "tapestry" becomes clear. The famine didn't just hit Egypt; it hit the land of Canaan where Joseph's father Jacob and his eleven brothers lived. If Joseph hadn't been in Egypt to store the grain, his entire family would have starved to death. There is a famous moment at the end of the story where Joseph confronts his brothers. Instead of seeking revenge, he says:

> **"You intended to harm me, but God intended it for good to accomplish what is now being done, the saving of many lives."**

Joseph realized that his life wasn't a series of accidents intended to make him rich or powerful; he was a tool used to keep a specific lineage alive. The "tapestry" wasn't about the beauty of the thread (Joseph); it was about the strength of the finished cloth (the survival of Israel).

Jacob's misery is a profound warning to believers who try

to use personal issues with a brother, sister, or family member to cut themselves off from the body God has spiritually joined them to. When he disconnected from his father's house (the place of the covenant promise given to Isaac and Abraham), he entered a period of exile, deception, and hardship (Genesis 29-31). He was away from the land, under the authority of a manipulative uncle (Laban), and despite gaining wealth and family, he was not in the place of God's full purpose. The blessing he stole was meant to position him as the covenant bearer for a nation, not just to prosper him as an individual. Before Joseph was sold into slavery, he shared a specific vision with his brothers:

> *"We were binding sheaves of grain out in the field when suddenly my sheaf rose and stood upright, while your sheaves gathered around mine and bowed down to it." (Genesis 37:7).*

The Prophetic Declaration was corporate, "May nations serve you and peoples bow down to you... May those who curse you be cursed and those who bless you be blessed." (Genesis 27:29). This was about the destiny of the nation of Israel, prefigured in Jacob.

The turning point from Jacob's wrestling with God is an indication of surrendering his personal feelings and will to the purpose and will of God. His limb was a sign and scar to remind him of the stubborn will and cunning ways from which he was delivered. Jacob's return to the land and his purpose culminated at the Jabbok River (Genesis 32:22-32). Here, fearing reconnection with Esau (his past sin and the threat to the promise), he wrestled with God himself. He refused to let go until he received a blessing. This was no longer about stealing a blessing for himself; it was about securing the destiny of the nation that would come from him.

A believer who willfully disconnects from the local expression of the Body of Christ (the church) disconnects from God's primary mechanism for growth, protection, and purpose. Hebrews 10:24-25: *"And let us consider how we may spur one another on toward love and good deeds, not giving up meeting together, as some are in the habit of doing, but encouraging one another..."* This separation leads to spiritual deadness, a lack of spiritual awareness, openness to false doctrine (Ephesians 4:14), and a loss of sense of purpose. Like Jacob in Haran, one can be "blessed" but not in the center of God's ultimate will. Judas was blessed to be in the company of Jesus and the other disciples, but Judas' concerns about money and the care of worldly things caused him to separate from the body. For thirty pieces of silver, Judas forfeited his position not only amongst the disciples, but also his seat in glory.

Outward signs of worldly wealth and success are not necessarily a sign of spiritual fulfillment and well-being, especially if the believer is cut off from where God has spiritually placed them. The spiritual encounters one experiences during times of separation from the body serve as a means of spiritual preservation, due to divine mercy, indicating God's love for the believer.

Moses' experience in the wilderness is a clear illustration of the need to return to the body in Egypt. Moses stands as one of the most pivotal figures in Scripture, a man chosen by God to lead His people from bondage to freedom and to establish them as a covenant nation. His life, like Joseph's, was marked by divine intervention, trials, and a calling that shaped the destiny of Israel.

Moses was born during a time of great oppression for the Israelites, who were enslaved in Egypt under Pharaoh's harsh rule. Fearing the growing population of the Israelites, Pharaoh decreed that all Hebrew male infants be killed. Yet, God's hand was upon Moses from the beginning. His mother, Jochebed, hid him for three months and then placed him in a basket among the reeds of the Nile. By divine providence, Pharaoh's daughter discovered him and raised him as her own, giving Moses a unique position as both a Hebrew and a member of Pharaoh's household.

Though raised in the luxury of Egypt's palace, Moses never forgot his Hebrew identity. As a young man, he witnessed the suffering of his people and, in a moment of anger, killed an Egyptian who was beating a Hebrew slave. Fearing for his life, Moses fled to the wilderness of Midian, where he spent 40 years as a shepherd. It was in this season of obscurity that God prepared Moses for his ultimate calling.

At the burning bush, God revealed Himself to Moses and called him to deliver the Israelites from slavery. Despite Moses' initial reluctance and feelings of inadequacy, God assured him, *"I will be with you"* (Exodus 3:12). Armed with God's promise and power, Moses returned to Egypt and confronted Pharaoh with the command, "Let my people go." Through a series of miraculous plagues, God demonstrated His sovereignty over Egypt's gods, culminating in the Passover and the Israelites' dramatic exodus through the parted Red Sea.

Moses served as a mediator, interceding for Israel when they rebelled and guiding them through the wilderness for 40 years. Despite their grumbling and disobedience, Moses remained faithful to his calling, though he himself was not permitted to enter the Promised Land.

Moses' life is a testament to God's power to use flawed and reluctant individuals for His purposes. From a helpless infant in a basket to the leader of a nation, Moses' journey reflects God's ability to redeem and transform. His story points to Christ, the ultimate Deliverer, who leads His people out of the bondage of sin and into the freedom of God's kingdom. For believers, Moses' life serves as a reminder that God's calling often comes with challenges, but His presence and power are sufficient. Like Moses, we are called to trust in God's plan, even when the path seems uncertain. Through Moses, God wove a thread of deliverance and covenant into His eternal tapestry, a pattern that continues to unfold in the lives of His people today. Spiritual attack had cut him off from where God intended him to be. His peace and joy were short-lived until he encountered God's burning bush, a place of restoration, healing, calling, and empowerment. Moses was destined to be a spiritual deliverer of God's people, not to tend sheep in the wilderness. Joseph was being cut off by the spirit of his brother, Jacob was being cut off by the spirit of his brother, Esau, and Moses was being cut off by the spirit of his adopted brother, Pharaoh's son, who was now the King of Egypt. Which spirit is preventing you from associating with the rest of the Body? It is your God intended place of spiritual assignment and empowerment. Like Joseph, you are not dreaming for yourself; you are dreaming for a people. Like Jacob, you are not wrestling to win; you are wrestling to be renamed. Like Moses, you are not hiding in exile; you are being called as a deliverer to those in bondage.

The spiritual encounters one experiences during times

of separation from the body serve as a means of spiritual preservation. Through divine mercy, these moments indicate God's profound love for the believer. Moses' experience in the wilderness is a clear illustration of this; while the desert provided a temporary refuge, he eventually had to return to the "body" in Egypt. A spiritual attack had cut him off from his true destination, leaving his peace and joy short-lived until he reached the burning bush—a place of restoration, healing, and empowerment.

Moses was destined to be a deliverer, not a shepherd in exile. Like Joseph and Jacob, he was being "cut off" by the spirit of a brother. I understand this sense of being "cut off" because I have walked that desert road myself.

***

My own began under the mentorship of my biological father. He was my inspiration, the spark that ignited God's calling on my life. When he passed away, I felt a deep, biting resentment toward God. I felt separated and cut off from the source of my inspiration. Yet, in that wilderness of grief, the Lord spoke a clear message of reassurance to me. In 1979, that encounter led me to rediscover my faith and fully accept Jesus as my Savior.

Just as God provided for Moses, He provided for me through people like Sister Rose Gabriel, the nun who looked past my circumstances to ensure my education continued at St. Patrick's High School. Even when I felt abandoned, God's favor was a shield. In 1989, this calling moved from the internal to the global. During the Liberian civil crisis—surrounded by spiritual battles and physical danger—I realized I wasn't just surviving; I was being preserved for a purpose.

Which spirit is preventing you from associating with the rest of the Body? Is it the spirit of abandonment, grief, or fear? Your current "wilderness" is not your destination; it is your place of assignment.

- Like Joseph, you are not dreaming for yourself; you are dreaming for people.
- Like Jacob, you are not wrestling to win; you are wrestling to be renamed.
- Like Moses—and like me—you are not hiding in exile; you are being called as a deliverer to those in bondage.

Chapter 4

Living the Spirit-Led Life

Ephesians 2:10

A tapestry is a skillfully woven artwork made up of thousands of single threads, colors, and styles. They are carefully decorated and very detailed in design. They are patterned one step at a time, with each step building upon the previous one. They are usually woven by a skilled weaver on a loom. In the divine realm, a tapestry represents the combined work of God in individual lives, across generations, and within the Body of Christ. "We are the workmanship of the Holy Spirit, created by the Father, in Christ Jesus for good works…" (Ephesians 2:10)

The making-up of a divine tapestry is a spirit-led act of God's masterwork in the life of a believer. It speaks to the structural and spiritual role of the Holy Spirit working in and through believers. The make-up of a Divine Tapestry consists of the threads, the weaving process, the loom of grace, and the presentation or final display. The patterns of the threads are the trails of the stories, seasons, and struggles of the believer's life.

"And we know that all things work together for good to those who love God..." (Romans 8:28).

The strands of threads also reveal a believer's personality, past (good and bad), gifts and grace, pain and persistence, and seasons of triumph in the wilderness. In a divine economy, every thread has a purpose; no thread is ever wasted. Even the dark-colored threads of sorrow and brokenness contribute to the depth and beauty of the divine image God is forming.

The Holy Spirit takes what was meant for harm and reweaves it for glory (Genesis 50:20). The thread of loss becomes the line of healing. The thread of rejection becomes the backdrop for divine favor. *"God made everything to be beautiful in its time"* (Ecclesiastes 3:11). In God's design, the cross of Christ and the covenants of God form the loom on which our lives are aligned and shaped. The characteristics of the divine loom are fixed in eternity (Hebrews 13:20). Its tension is necessary. Its trials help to form character and structure in the lives of believers (James 1:2–4). Heaven holds the warp, the vertical threads, and the Holy Spirit guides the weft, the horizontal threads. Tension is not accidental; it's necessary for weaving. Suffering and glory are not opposites; they are connected realities (Romans 8:17–18). *"The Spirit Himself bears witness… intercedes… and works all things…"* (Romans 8:26–28). The Holy Spirit is the Master Weaver, the unseen hand of God actively arranging, twisting together, and connecting every element of a believer's life into the image of Christ. The Holy Spirit weaves conviction into transformation, pain into promise and empowerment, delay into development, and prophetic promises into appointed seasons. Sometimes, a person can only see the back side of the tapestry: knots, tangles, chaos. The Spirit sees the front, a masterpiece in the making. The pattern is "Christ in you, the hope of glory."

> *"For whom the Holy Spirit foreknew, He also predestined that person to be conformed to the image of His Son…"* (Romans 8:29).

God does not weave a casual design. The pattern is consistent, the image of Jesus. Everything in a believer's life is being aligned to God's eternal blueprint, the transformation into

Christlikeness, a from glory-to-glory progression (2 Corinthians 3:18) in unity with the whole body. The tapestry is collective, not just individual. Believers are not being remade into a better version of themselves; they are being woven into the body, exact imprint and DNA of the firstborn son. A believer's existence and life's experiences are often described as a journey or a passage through layers of spiritual elevations. These elevations give meaning, identity, and purpose to the calling of God in the life of the believer. Each layer is distinct yet interconnected in a person's life. Spiritually, irrespective of culture or tradition, each layer is linked with a vision that points to realities beyond the visible world. These visions, sometimes simple and sometimes overelaborate in dreams and imagery, are filled with revelations and spiritual meaning, often serving as doorways to more profound truths. Each vision embodies a distinct aspect of their life's unfolding narrative. A believer is called by God, anointed to function, empowered to fulfill their purpose, and favored for any occasion. When woven together, these elements of the Holy Spirit in a believer's life create a profound tapestry or embroidery that defines their individual and collective features and futures.

I must tell you—I wasn't always the first to jump when I heard the call. In fact, there was a time in Bible school when I tried to 'help' God along with a little bit of manipulation. As I previously mentioned, a sign-up sheet for the mission field had been sitting at the front of our classroom for weeks. It was white, blank, and frankly, embarrassing. Every day I walked past it; I felt this mounting frustration. Not because I wanted to go, I was terrified of the mission field—but because I hated that no one else was signing up.

So, I hatched a plan. It was a bit of a trick, really. I thought, 'If I put my name down, my friends will see it and feel inspired (or maybe just guilty) to sign up too. Then, on the very last day, I'll just quietly slip back up there and scratch my name off.' I felt so clever. I signed that paper with a smile, thinking I was doing everyone a favor. But here is the thing about God: He has a very particular, almost humorous way of calling you. I went back to that classroom on the final day, ready to perform my 'great escape,' only to find the list was gone. My name was the only one on it. The deadline had been moved up, the paper collected, and the 'joke' was officially on me.

In that moment, looking at the empty space where the list used to be, I didn't feel a bolt of lightning. I felt a quiet, divine chuckle. It was as if the Lord was saying, "Nice try, but I've got you." I realized then that while I was busy trying to lure my friends, God had already lured me.

Like Joseph, you are not dreaming for yourself; you are dreaming for a people. Like Jacob, you are not wrestling to win; you are wrestling to be renamed. Like Moses, you are not hiding in exile; you are being called as a deliverer to those in bondage.

Chapter 5

The Four Elements of a Divine Calling

1 Corinthians 15:10

"But what I am I am by the grace of God, and His grace bestowed upon me did not prove ineffectual. But I labored more strenuously than all the rest, yet it was not I, but God's grace working with me." (1 Corinthians 15:10 (Weymouth New Testament))

The Apostle Paul, in this passage, recounts his spiritual journey from the moment the father first identified him to be the person he is now and the position he was appointed to as an apostle. He told his account, detailing all his struggles and achievements, both spiritual and physical. He stressed that it was the power of God, through divine guidance, that actually made this life possible. He concluded with four fascinating but spiritually profound acknowledgements:

1) His foundational belief and affirmation of God were without any fault in Him – (*But what I am I am by the grace of God*)

2) His acknowledgement of God's favor at work was without any disappointment – (*and His grace bestowed upon me did not prove ineffectual*)

3) The confidence and resilience he applied personally were through natural efforts due to his faith in Jesus – *("But I labored more strenuously than all the rest")*

4) His bottom-line conviction and conclusion was that grace had produced humility in him – *(Yet it was not I, but*

God's grace working with me)

The Apostle Paul's revelation, "But what I am I am, by the grace of God…," was not said in boast or defame, but said in character, integrity, faithfulness, and humility. Divine revelation will lead to spiritual vision, and vision, sometimes simple and sometimes overelaborate in dreams and imagery, is filled with revelations and spiritual meaning. They often serve as doorways to more profound truths. Thus, this affirmation by the apostle reveals four essential elements that depict The Calling and Empowerment of a Believer: **The Person, The Vessel, The Mantle, and The Grace**, as a Living Tapestry of The Holy Spirit.

These four elements frequently emerge as indications in visions. Recognizing these four elements not only deepens a believer's spiritual insight but also throws light on the ways by which believers are called, equipped, empowered, and preserved in fulfilling God's purpose. In the economy of God, encounters with the Holy Spirit and divine assignments are two spiritual impacts that are not accidental. They follow a heavenly pattern and design, which flows from The Person, to The Vessel, to The Mantle, and to Grace. It reveals the progressive unveiling of a life ordained for divine achievements. Each believer, in God's plan, is called to a unique mission marked by divine encounters and the empowerment of the Holy Spirit. These four elements lead a believer to search deeply into the riches of Heaven, experiencing how God chooses, fashions, anoints, and enables ordinary individuals to fulfill extraordinary purposes. Such spiritual experience reveals the dynamic interplay between one's spiritual identity, readiness, anointing, and divine assignment, as well as the sustaining power of grace. A believer is first chosen as a person, then formed into a vessel, clothed with a mantle, and finally sustained by grace. Life unfolds in seasons. But for the spirit-led believer, it is not time that rules; it is grace. Grace is not passive; it is a divine scheduler.

The Person

> *"For we are God's workmanship...in Christ Jesus... prepared beforehand..." (Ephesians 2:10)*

In the grand scheme of God, choice and function in a tapestry symbolize not only beauty but purposeful design. It is a combination of lives, seasons, struggles, and victories, woven together by the Holy Spirit. The most important element in this divine tapestry is the "Person." The "Person" is usually an individual selected, called, and empowered by the Spirit to function in the Body of Christ and fulfill Heaven's intention on earth. The person is not merely a thread but the starting point of a weave. They are identified by God, set apart for a purpose, and empowered by grace. Specifically, in the cases of Moses, David, and Paul, you will recognize that spiritually, they had multiple disqualifiers against them.

David and Paul, two of the most significant figures in Scripture, both had moments in their lives that could be seen as spiritual disqualifiers, yet God's grace and purpose prevailed. David, known as "a man after God's own heart" (1 Samuel 13:14), faced several moral and personal failures. He committed adultery with Bathsheba and, to cover his sin, orchestrated the murder of her husband, Uriah (2 Samuel 11). As a father, David struggled to address the sins and conflicts within his family, including the rape of his daughter Tamar and the rebellion of his son Absalom (2 Samuel 13–18). Additionally, his decision to take a census of Israel, driven by pride, brought judgment upon the nation (2 Samuel 24). Despite these failures, David's heartfelt repentance, as seen in Psalm 51, and his unwavering faith in God allowed him to be restored and used mightily. His life became a testament to God's redemptive power, and through his lineage came the Messiah, Jesus Christ.

Paul, formerly known as Saul, also had a past that seemed to disqualify him from God's service. Before his dramatic conversion, Paul was a zealous Pharisee who actively persecuted the early church. He approved of the stoning of Stephen, the first Christian martyr, and sought to imprison and harm followers of Jesus (Acts 8:1–3; Acts 9:1–2). Paul later described himself as a "blasphemer, persecutor, and insolent opponent" of Christ (1 Timothy 1:13). Even after his conversion, Paul faced criticism for his unimpressive physical presence and speaking abilities, which some in the Corinthian church mocked (2 Corinthians 10:10). Additionally, he endured a persistent "thorn in the flesh," a weakness or affliction that reminded him of his dependence on God's grace (2 Corinthians 12:7–9). Yet, despite these challenges, Paul experienced a radical transformation on the road to Damascus (Acts 9:3–19) and became one of the most influential apostles, spreading the gospel to the Gentiles and writing much of the New Testament.

Both David and Paul demonstrate that God's calling is not based on human merit but on His sovereign grace. Their lives, marked by failure and weakness, were redeemed and woven into God's divine plan. David's moral failures and family struggles, and Paul's violent opposition to the church, could have disqualified them in the eyes of men. Yet, God used David to establish the royal lineage of Christ and Paul to carry the gospel to the nations. Their stories remind us that God's grace is sufficient, and His power is made perfect in weakness (2 Corinthians 12:9).

If Moses, David or Paul were in our time, we would have branded them unholy and unfit as a divine choice. But the Spirit of God strategically selected them for Holy assignment. God was not looking at their Holiness, because they were not at the time of choosing. But the Lord saw their audacity, aptness, agility, and availability in their preparedness for spiritual confrontations.

God selects the Person known before time. Before you were formed by God in the womb, He knew you. Before you were born, He sanctified you. (Jeremiah 1:5). So, if God knew these people before time, before they were formed and born, then, even in their flaws and early mistakes, they were still God's favorites.

> *"...For the gifts and calling of God are without repentance" (Romans 11:29)*

The NKJV says, "...For the gifts and calling of God are irrevocable." God does not change his mind. The choice of God is made before the person is formed. God's selection is based on internal identity; God doesn't randomly assign roles. He selects individuals based on his eternal pattern woven into their spiritual DNA. There couldn't have been anyone else in the Holy Spirit's tapestry more qualified than them. God looks at divine qualities in natural vessels before qualification. God marks purpose before calling, "Those He predestined, He also called…" (Romans 8:30). The calling of the person is the Holy Spirit awakening the preordained identity to function in divine purpose. Calling aligns the person with their God-intended role in the Body of Christ and their assignment in the Kingdom of God. It is not just ministry as usual; it's divinely operating in the gifts of the Holy Spirit, such as being a warrior, a healer, a builder, a prophet, an intercessor, a teacher, or a kingdom financier, among others. A calling is often confirmed through visions, anointing, prophetic utterances, or a divine encounter. The Holy Spirit stirs deep within, revealing what's written in the tapestry according to the weaving of the loom of God (Psalm 139:16).

> *"…But His grace to me was not in vain… I labored more strenuously… yet not I, but the grace of God with me" (1 Corinthians 15:10).*

Empowerment is where the grace of God meets the selection and calling and releases divine capacity. Grace is not only a favor, it is fuel for awakening the fire. It activates gifts, endurance, strategy, spiritual authority, and effectiveness beyond human strength. In the tapestry of the spirit, no two threads are alike. Your color, placement and texture all serve Heaven's design. When a person accepts their selection, embraces their calling, and walks in empowerment, they become a visible expression of Christ in the fabric of the Church. All believers are being transformed into Christ's nature (2 Corinthians 3:18); "Christ in you, the hope of glory." (Colossians 1:27). The tapestry is not about showcasing people; it's about revealing Jesus through each person. The person becomes the canvas for the image of Jesus, not a self-improvement, but a Spirit-led transformation.

The Vessel

2 Corinthians 4:7

The next dimension in "The Four Elements of Divine Calling and Empowerment" is the vessel, the person shaped and conditioned for service. Paul writes, "But we have this treasure in earthen vessels, that the excellence of the power may be of God and not of us" (2 Corinthians 4:7). The vessel speaks of readiness, consecration, and humility. Preparation is both inward and outward. In 2 Timothy 2:20-21, Paul draws a clear image:

> **"But in a great house there are not only vessels of gold and silver, but also of wood and clay, some for honor and some for dishonor. Therefore, if anyone cleanses himself from the latter, he will be a vessel for honor, sanctified and useful for the Master, prepared for every good work."**

Holiness is not optional for those desiring to carry the weight of God's glory. This cleansing is not a matter of self-effort alone, but rather the ongoing work of the Spirit, convicting, purifying, and empowering. The vessel is also the channel through which spiritual gifts flow. The gifts of the Spirit, prophecy, healing, tongues, discerning of spirits, flow powerfully through vessels who are surrendered and emptied of self (1 Thessalonians 5:19). Yieldedness is the stance through which the Spirit's power is most fully revealed. If the person is the core, the vessel is the structure that supports it. The structure is the body, mind, and spirit, contained and expressing the life of the Holy Spirit within. The Vessel holds the potential and the limitations of being alive and spiritually productive. It is shaped not just by human genes or environment, but by choices, discipline, and openness to transformation.

A vessel is a life, a spirit, a soul, and a body. Vessels are often portrayed as cups, jars, or ships, objects that carry or pour out their contents. It is an object that endures pain through heat and fire when cleansing and refining; pressure when stretching, forming, and shaping; and discipline and patience when widening and deepening for purpose. Spiritually, the Vessel is prepared to receive. It is made ready for a purpose, whether through discipline, suffering, or joy. The process of becoming a vessel often involves cleansing by piercing fingers, strengthening by refining fire, forming by shaping tough hands, and filling by pouring of sour, bitter, or sweet liquid or solid objects. When grace (the gifts of the Holy Spirit) is mixed with those objects and stirred together, the outcome is an unbelievable and incredible taste and outpouring (Revelation 10:9). It is a spiritual emptying of old contents (beliefs and wounds) to make room for divine wisdom, power and purpose. The process by which a vessel is shaped is both deliberate and mysterious. The adversities a believer endures, the lessons they learn during those spiritual encounters, and the experiences, all these are the tools of the Master Potter, forming the vessel for the spiritual conditions that lie ahead. A vessel may crack under pressure; yet, even in brokenness, there is beauty. Kintsugi is the Japanese art of repairing broken pottery by joining pieces back together and filling cracks with lacquer dusted with powdered gold, silver, or platinum, thereby highlighting the flaws in the mended object.

This art teaches believers that scars can become our greatest strengths, transforming wounds into windows of grace.

Every vessel has a capacity, a limit to what it can hold. Recognizing one's limitations is a form of wisdom; it is the humility that admits need and the courage that seeks help. Yet, vessels can stretch and grow. A believer's capacity to serve, love, give, understand, and endure can be expanded. As we are shaped, so too are we expanded, able to carry more than we once imagined. The vessel represents the condition and readiness of the person to carry spiritual weight and responsibility. The vessel represents the process of formation. Clay must be shaped, refined, and even broken if it resists the Potter's hand. A person becomes a vessel when they yield to the shaping, pruning, and refining of the Holy Spirit. Spiritually, this is where deliverance, inner healing, and sanctification often play out. You may be called, but until you are processed, you are not yet ready to carry the weight of the mantle.

God is not looking for perfect vessels, but for yielded ones. Vessels are tested not only in their formation, but in their capacity to carry glory without leaking or cracking under pressure. Anointing flows through consecrated vessels. Power without process leads to collapse. Processed vessels can carry weighty mantles without breaking. A vessel must be sanctified to hold pure contents and strong enough to withstand the pressure of its anointing. The Spirit's baptism (Acts 1:5) is the divine act of filling the prepared vessel. Speaking in tongues is the initial evidence (Acts 2:4) of this infilling, but the purpose is empowerment for service. The Vessel is not the source of power; it is the carrier of the "treasure," who is Christ Himself. The spiritual gifts (1 Corinthians 12:7-11) are the various ways the treasure within the vessel is manifested to the world.

The Mantle

1 Kings 19:13-19

13 So it was, when Elijah heard it, that he wrapped his face in his mantle and went out and stood in the entrance of the cave. Suddenly a voice came to him, and said, "What are you doing here, Elijah?"

14 And he said, "I have been very zealous for the Lord God of hosts; because the children of Israel have forsaken Your covenant, torn down Your altars, and killed Your prophets with the sword. I alone am left; and they seek to take my life."

15 Then the Lord said to him: "Go, return on your way to the Wilderness of Damascus; and when you arrive, anoint Hazael as
king over Syria. 16 Also you shall anoint Jehu the son of Nimshi
as king over Israel. And Elisha the son of Shaphat of Abel
Meholah you shall anoint as prophet in your place. 17 It shall
be that whoever escapes the sword of Hazael, Jehu will kill; and
whoever escapes the sword of Jehu, Elisha will kill. 18 Yet I have
reserved seven thousand in Israel, all whose knees have not bowed to Baal, and every mouth that has not kissed him."

Elisha Follows Elijah

19 So he departed from there, and found Elisha the son of Shaphat, who was plowing with twelve yoke of oxen before him, and he was with the twelfth. Then Elijah passed by him and threw his mantle on him.

The Mantle is a spiritual covering, not necessarily a cloak, cloth, or garment. It is Heaven's assignment and the weight of its anointing, mandate, and responsibilities bestowed on an individual. *"So he departed from there, and found Elisha… and threw his mantle on him". (1 Kings 19:19).* The mantle is the symbol of your divine assignment, your spiritual authority, and the weight of responsibility placed upon your life. It symbolizes the specific calling you carry from heaven. Examples of mantles include Elijah's prophetic mantle (1 Kings 19:13), Joseph's coat of many colors, which represented favor and destiny (Genesis 37:3), and Jesus' seamless garment, anointing of unity and kingship (John 19:23). Every mantle is unique, custom-designed by heaven. You must be processed before you are mantled. The Spirit imparts power, but the mantle calls for the right conduct or behavior.

The mantle is a representation of authority, purpose, and anointing. In ancient cultures, a mantle was a physical garment, often laid or placed upon the shoulders of leaders or prophets to signify their role. In other words, to "pick up the mantle" is to assume responsibility, to step into a role that surpasses mere self-interest. The mantle is usually conferred after preparation; a vessel must be ready, and a person must be willing. It is not chosen lightly, nor is it always comfortable. The mantle confers both honor and weight, for with anointing there is the burden of expectation and the certainty of challenge. Some run from the mantle, while others seek it, but in truth, it is given as much as it is chosen.

There is a spiritual grace or holiness in the moment one receives the mantle. It may come as a formal ceremony, such as a promotion, an induction, or an ordination, or it may be transferred solemnly, in a moment of realization or necessity. Whatever the form, the mantle marks a transition from preparation to action, from simply being to actually doing. Bearing this conferment is a holy commitment that is more than assuming a title for the sake of a position; it is accepting the weight of a sacred duty to serve, lead, create, or heal. This, in most cases, requires sacrificing comfort, personal ambition, and even safety. Yet, it is in shouldering the mantle that one discovers the true measure of one's character and calling. To bear the mantle is to be on a divine mission or assignment.

A tangible impartation of authority and responsibility often marks this. In Scripture, the mantle is a symbol of prophetic succession and empowerment. Consider Elijah and Elisha: "Then Elijah took his mantle, rolled it up, and struck the water; and it was divided this way and that, so that the two of them crossed over on dry ground... Then Elijah said to Elisha, 'Ask! What may I do for you, before I am taken away from you?' Elisha said, 'Please let a double portion of your spirit be upon me'... Then he took the mantle of Elijah that had fallen from him, and struck the water… and it was divided" (2 Kings 2:8-14).

In this passage from 2 Kings, we witness a profound "passing of the torch" (or in this case, the mantle) from the prophet Elijah to his successor, Elisha. By striking the Jordan River to part the waters, Elijah demonstrates that his authority comes from a divine source. Knowing his time on Earth is ending, he offers Elisha a final request; Elisha asks for a "double portion" of his spirit—not out of greed, but as a request to be recognized as the legitimate heir and firstborn spiritual son. When Elisha later uses the fallen mantle to part the waters himself, it serves as a miraculous "receipt," proving to both Elisha and all observers that the same power and divine favor that rested on Elijah had successfully transferred to him.

The mantle is not self-assumed; It is received through closeness, faithfulness, and spiritual hunger. Elisha's pursuit of Elijah is illustrative of the disciple's pursuit of God's presence and power. In a spiritual experience, mantles may be imparted through prophetic acts, the laying on of hands, and divine encounters. The Holy Spirit himself is the great Mantle-bearer, clothing the believer with "power from on high" (Luke 24:49). Yet, mantles are not only for gift bearers or spiritual leaders. Every believer is called to a surrounding of influence, in ministry, the marketplace, or the mission field. The mantle represents Divine empowerment to serve, speak, heal, influence, and lead. Carrying a mantle is both a privilege and a burden, requiring a complete reliance on the Spirit. David was anointed three times before he sat on the throne; each mantle prepared him for another level of service.

Spiritually, the mantle is a heavenly treasure, gifted by the Holy Spirit to an individual, yet controlled and directed by the Holy Spirit in conferring and use. Daniel makes it clear in Daniel 5:24-28 that God sent a hand to write a message to the King of Babylon. The hand signifies that God is able to anoint any messenger to carry out a divine assignment. It was a symbol of divine interruption and authority. It signifies that God is ever-present, and His dominion extends over every nation. His sovereignty extends to every ruler, country, and people. Even in the pagan nation of Babylon, God's rule was evident. This reveals the sovereign and majestic rule of God: His kingdom is over all kingdoms. The "hand" wasn't God Himself, but rather a divine agent sent on a specific assignment. Just as God sends angels, prophets, and people, he also sends judgments. The misuse of the temple vessels was a symbolically grave offense.

These vessels were sanctified, set apart for worshipping and glorifying God, and were Holy unto the Lord. This is also true for a Divine mantle. Using what is sacred unto the Lord for unholy purposes, especially to glorify idols, is an act of spiritual treason. Belshazzar violated sacred boundaries, bringing truth and error into an unholy alliance. This reflects the modern-day disregard for holiness, where many blend truth with error, the Spirit with the flesh, and holy purposes with carnal ambition. Just as vessels can be misused, so can the mantle, gifts of the Spirit, financial blessings, and sacred callings. When the holy things of God are manipulated for entertainment, profit, or ego, the fear of the Lord departs, and judgment is near.

Judges 6:12-16 (NKJV)

12) And the angel of the Lord appeared to him, and said to him, "The Lord is with you, you mighty man of valor!" 13) Gideon said to him, "O [a]my lord, if the Lord is with us, why then has all this happened to us? And where are all His miracles which our fathers told us about, saying, 'Did not the Lord bring us up from Egypt?' But now the Lord has forsaken us and delivered us into the hands of the Midianites." 14) Then the Lord turned to him and said, "Go in this might of yours, and you shall save Israel from the hand of the Midianites. Have I not sent you?" 15) So he said to him, "O [b]my Lord, how can I save Israel? Indeed my clan is the weakest in Manasseh, and I am the least in my father's house." 16) And the Lord said to him, "Surely I will be with you, and you shall [c]defeat the Midianites as one man."

1 Samuel 16:6-13 (NKJV)

6) So it was, when they came, that he looked at Eliab and said, "Surely the Lord's anointed is before Him!" 7) But the Lord said to Samuel, "Do not look at his appearance or at his physical stature, because I have [a]refused him. For[b] the Lord does not see as man sees; for man looks at the outward appearance, but the Lord looks at the heart." 8) So Jesse called Abinadab, and made him pass before Samuel. And he said, "Neither has the Lord chosen this one." 9) Then Jesse made Shammah pass by. And he said, "Neither has the Lord chosen this one." 10) Thus Jesse made seven of his sons pass before Samuel. And Samuel said to Jesse, "The Lord has not chosen these." 11) And Samuel said to Jesse, "Are all the young men here?" Then he said, "There remains yet the youngest, and there he is, keeping the sheep." And Samuel said to Jesse, "Send and bring him. For we will not [c]sit down till he comes here." 12) So he sent and brought him in. Now he was ruddy, with [d]bright eyes, and good-looking. And the Lord said, "Arise, anoint him; for this is the one!" 13) Then Samuel took the horn of oil and anointed him in the midst of his brothers; and the Spirit of the Lord came upon David from that day forward. So Samuel arose and went to Ramah.

Grace

1 Corinthians 15:10

"But by the grace of God I am what I am, and his grace toward me was not in vain.

Grace is the God enabler that supports and sustains a believer. It is the divine oxygen of every called and anointed life. Without grace, the person fails, the vessel cracks, and the mantle remains unproductive. It is the divine thread that holds the tapestry of a believer's life together. Grace is the strand from the Holy Spirit that weaves through the person, strengthens the vessel, and empowers the mantle. Though it is undeserved, it is always abundant and sufficient in supply. It is the golden fiber of the blood of Jesus that runs through every believer's life. The Apostle Paul described it this way: *"I labored... yet not I, but the grace of God which was with me"* (1 Corinthians 15:10). Grace empowers the believer to shine, endure, and contribute beyond their natural capacity. It weaves redemption into a believer's personhood, supernatural strength into their vessel, the Oil of anointing into their mantle, and God's Glory into their life's story.

"My grace is sufficient for you, for My strength is made perfect in weakness" (2 Corinthians 12:9). Grace is not just God granting mercy; it is a divine power source. It does not ignore spiritual flaws, but transforms them into testimonies and witnesses (1 Corinthians 15:9).

Grace is the Holy Spirit's empowerment beyond the self in the person. It is the most mysterious of the four elements of divine calling. If the person is the root, the vessel is the form, and the mantle is the purpose, then the grace is the empowering force. It is the wind in the sails, the oil in the lamp, the breath that invigorates. Grace is that favor which comes unearned, unexpected, and often unexplained. It is the favor of God that opens doors, the strength that sustains in times of weakness, and the inspiration that triggers wisdom and endurance. Some call it luck, while others refer to it as human intelligence or fate, but believers recognize it as divine intervention through special favor and assistance. Whatever the name, grace is the difference between struggling and rising in Christ. If the person is to be chosen, the vessel is to be prepared, and the mantle is to be bestowed, then grace is the enabling power that assists and sustains them all. In spiritual understanding, grace is not merely unearned favor but the Spirit's empowerment for triumphant living. Paul, the apostle of grace, wrote, "*But by the grace of God I am what I am, and His grace toward me was not in vain; but I labored more abundantly than they all, yet not I, but the grace of God which was with me*" (1 Corinthians 15:10).

The lives of Peter, Paul, and Stephen vividly illustrate how God's grace covers failures, strengthens in weakness, and empowers believers to reflect Christ. Peter, one of Jesus' closest disciples, experienced a profound failure when he denied Christ three times on the night of His arrest (Luke 22:54–62). Yet, after His resurrection, Jesus restored Peter with grace, reaffirming his calling to shepherd His people (John 21:15–19). Paul, once a fierce persecutor of the church, was transformed by grace on the road to Damascus and became a powerful apostle to the Gentiles. Even in his ministry, Paul faced a "thorn in the flesh," a persistent weakness or affliction, but he testified that God's grace was sufficient and His power was made perfect in weakness (2 Corinthians 12:9). Stephen, the first Christian martyr, demonstrated the empowering nature of grace as he forgave his persecutors even while being stoned to death, echoing the words of Christ by praying, "Lord, do not hold this sin against them" (Acts 7:60). In each of these lives, grace not only covered their failures and weaknesses but also activated their success in fulfilling God's purposes, showing that His grace is the foundation of restoration, strength, and forgiveness. Grace covers failures and activates success.

It was grace that restored Peter after his failure; grace that strengthens Paul in weakness; grace that empowers Stephen to forgive his persecutors. The Holy Spirit's work is a work of grace: "My grace is sufficient for you, for My strength is made perfect in weakness" (2 Corinthians 12:9). A spirit-filled believer places great emphasis on the manifest presence of the Holy Spirit. Grace is experienced as physical power, the " spiritual magnetisms" or gifts from above. Healing, deliverance, prophecy, and miracles are not preserved for a spiritually selected few but the inheritance of every Spirit-filled believer. Grace makes the supernatural of the Holy Spirit available to everyone. Grace is not demanded; it is a favor delivered through love to be experienced by believers. It appears in moments of surrender, when the person is tired, the vessel is dry, and the mantle feels too burdensome. It fills the gap where self-effort ends, offering new hope, clarity, and possibility. Noteworthy figures in scripture, life, and the faith all testify to moments when grace transformed their struggles into triumph and despair into joy. To live in grace is to be humble and grateful. It is to recognize that every gift, every success, every act of kindness is in some way touched by the Spirit of God beyond natural control. Grace inspires generosity and compassion, enabling believers to forgive, connect, and dare great things. The Person, The Vessel, The Mantle, and The Grace are not isolated stages or elements, but rather a woven romance. Each informs, shapes, and elevates the others. We are called first to know ourselves, then to be shaped for a purpose, to lay hold of our anointing, and finally, to move forward not by our strength alone, but empowered by God's love. In the tapestry of each life, there are seasons where one element is the focus of emphasis. In the search for identity, it is the Person. In the shaping of capacity, it is the Vessel. In carrying the weight of the calling, it is the Mantle. And in the outpouring of love, it is grace. Yet, it is in their union that a believer becomes fully alive: authentic in personhood, firm in vessel, purposeful in mantle, and radiant in grace that lifts and sustains us. Finally, the romance is both personal and collective, a love story that resonates in every heart, a script written in every life, and a moment celebrated in every act of faith, compassion, and hope.

Ephesians 2:8-10 (NKJV)

8 For by grace you have been saved through faith, and that not of yourselves; it is the gift of God, 9 not of works, lest anyone should boast. 10 For we are His workmanship, created in Christ Jesus for good works, which God prepared beforehand that we should walk in them.

Romans 5:17 (NKJV)

17 For if by the one man's offense death reigned through the one, much more those who receive abundance of grace and of the gift of righteousness will reign in life through the One, Jesus Christ.)

Ephesians 2:10 (NKJV)

10 For we are His workmanship, created in Christ Jesus for good works, which God prepared beforehand that we should walk in them.

God chooses the person, the vessel is prepared through surrender and sanctification, the mantle is received as a divine assignment, and grace is the empowering presence that makes all things possible. Identity without surrender leads to pride;

surrender without assignment leads to aimlessness; assignment without empowerment leads to burnout. But when all four are present, the believer walks in fullness. Moses, though hesitant yet humble, became a deliverer because the grace of "I AM" was with him. Mary, overshadowed by the Spirit, became the vessel for the incarnation of Christ. Esther, whom we will learn about shortly, chosen for such a time as this, receives favor to save a nation. The spirit-filled life is a continual yielding, being shaped as a vessel, seeking God for fresh mantles, and living daily in the sufficiency of grace. The spirit-filled believer is marked by expectancy, hunger and boldness to participate in the supernatural.

"We are His workmanship, created in Christ Jesus for good works..." (Ephesians 2:10).

A tapestry appears disordered from the back, with tangled threads and uneven textures, but the front reveals a masterpiece. God, the Master Weaver, is using: Your person (identity), your vessel (capacity), your mantle (assignment), and his grace (empowerment) to weave something eternally glorious. What feels like delays, denials, or defeats is simply the weaving process. You are not breaking apart, you are becoming. The journey from person to vessel to mantle to grace is the story of every believer yielded to the Spirit. It is a journey marked by God's initiative, believers' obedience, his impartation, and his keeping power. As believers respond to the voice of the Holy Spirit, they will also be found ready and available as persons known by God, vessels prepared for honor, mantle-bearers for their generation, and carriers of grace to a world in need.

Paul prayed, *"That the God of our Lord Jesus Christ, the*

Father of glory, may give to you the spirit of wisdom and revelation in the knowledge of Him... and what is the exceeding greatness of His power toward us who believe" (Ephesians 1:17, 19)

Chapter 6

The Divine Tapestry of Purpose

Romans 13:11

11 And do this, knowing the time, that now it is high time to awake out of sleep; for now our salvation is nearer than when we first believed.

- *"...it is high time to awake out of sleep..."*

This passage issues a strong and crucial call to believers to encourage spiritual consciousness. The Apostle Paul's stirring appeal in Romans 13:11 resounds like a trumpet blast to a slumbering Church. This declaration is a strong request from the Spirit of God, through the Apostle Paul, for something spiritual to take place; otherwise, a window of spiritual opportunity will be closed, and a spiritually severe condition could take place. It implies a loud, clear, and pressing command to the Church and all believers. This call can be likened to the blowing of a trumpet in ancient times, demanding a swift and faithful response to halt certain behaviors and take the necessary course of action. It is a prophetic, timely, and strategic spiritual call. It calls the believer to rise from idleness towards spiritual assignments and align their priorities according to the divine timeline. This alignment to the divine timeline is woven into the tapestry of the loom of eternity. From a divine perspective, this is not only a call to awareness but to impact. An impact driven by divine alignment, spiritual awakening, and prophetic movement that the Spirit of God urgently requires. It is a call of God to the churches and all believers, similar to that in Revelation 1-4.

"Awake" in the Greek language from which this word comes means "to raise, to awaken, to provoke abruptly from sleep or inactivity." The connotation is one of resurrection power, spiritual alertness, and a divine activation. The word "awaken" is often used to describe resurrection from the dead, which implies that to "awake" is to shift from a death-like inactivity to dynamic life and divine usefulness. In this book, I refer to the Loom as a sacred instrument. A loom is a tool that weaves individual threads into a well-organized, patterned, and purposeful fabric. Spiritually, God is the Master Weaver in use of this Loom, and his church is the living tapestry he has designed. The Warp of the loom is the vertical threads that hold in tension or firmly in place, the unchanging standard of God's Word, His covenant, and eternal purposes. The Weft or horizontal threads woven through are the lives of believers, ministries, callings, and destinies brought into alignment with Heaven's structure. Together, they form the Divine Tapestry of Purpose, where every awakened believer is a vital thread.

A sleeping church is a crisis of spiritual unawareness. To be asleep spiritually is: (1) To lose sensitivity to the Spirit (1 Thessalonians 5:6); (2) To forget divine assignment (Judges 16:20) Samson "knew not that the LORD had departed"); (3) To neglect the hour of visitation (Luke 19:44); To cease watching and praying (Matthew 26:40–41). In a time of global shaking, to remain asleep is to risk being woven out of the tapestry. The impact of the Church hangs on her alertness. When believers slumber, the loom pauses. But when they awaken, the threads align again for Kingdom expansion.

Romans 13:11

11 And do this, knowing the time, that now it is high time to awake out of sleep; for now our salvation is nearer than when we first believed.

Spiritually, "Divine awakening" is usually marked by prophetic insight (Acts 2:17 – dreams and visions), spiritual boldness (Acts 4:31), Kingdom mobilization (Joel 2:1 – "Blow the trumpet…sound an alarm…"), and the fire of the Holy Spirit (Romans 12:11 – "fervent in spirit, serving the Lord"). To awaken is to come into harmony with the flow of the loom. God does not weave random patterns. Each thread (life, gift, calling) must be intentionally placed to complete the masterpiece. Impact happens when: (1) The thread is untangled (surrendered); (2) The pattern is recognized (discerned); (3) The process is welcomed and accepted (embraced); (4) The tension is borne (endured); and (5) The final product is celebrated.

Joseph was a thread awakened in the Loom. Joseph's story (Genesis 37–50) illustrates a man awakened for impact through trial, alignment, and vision. He was laced and stretched out like a thread, stripped, and prepared for the loom. His robe was taken, and his identity refined. He was pushed as a thread on a spool being thrown to roll aimlessly and stretched. He was thrown into a pit and prison with stress and tension applied to his life. He was thrust like a thread to be aligned into Pharaoh's court to be assigned and positioned. He was trusted as a chosen thread woven in its place and used by God to preserve nations. Through Joseph, a nation was saved, and the continuity of God's covenant tapestry was preserved. What appeared to be a separation from family was, in fact, a placement in the loom of destiny.

Believers are awakened for one purpose: to have an

impact. "It is high time…" (Romans 13:11). This phrase speaks of "Kairos," a divine moment where urgency meets opportunity. It is not ordinary time (Chronos), but a spiritually strategic time, a time pregnant with divine possibility.

To "awake for impact" is to: (1) Recognize the time by discerning prophetic seasons (1 Chronicles 12:32); (2) Refuse the worldly dreams and ambitions of the human society. Believers are not to sleep in compromise or convenience: (3) Return to Kingdom purpose to have their gifts, voice, and calling, realigned; (4) Reconnect with the rest of the "Body." All believers are one thread; impact requires unity; (5) Reignite your fire, stir up the gift within (2 Timothy 1:6).

The tapestry of impact runs from a simple thread to a credible witness with powerful testimonies. Each believer is called to be:

A) A thread of healing in a broken world
B) A thread of prophecy in a confused generation
C) A thread of holiness in a society with a culture of compromise
D) A thread of power in a highly religious society; and
E) A thread of love in an environment of hate and division.

Only when awakened and surrendered to the Divine Loom can believers' lives create a lasting spiritual impact. Romans 13:11 is not a suggestion; it is a commission. It's time to rise from religious routine, awaken from the drowsiness of the world, and submit to the hand of the Master Weaver. Let the Divine Loom turn again. Let the impact of awakened lives echo through the earth. Awaken for Impact, Rise, Align, and Impact. You are a Blood bought, Blood washed, and Precious possession, a Chosen Thread in the Tapestry of a Divine Loom.

Awakening for Impact

Acts 2:14-18 (NIV)

Then Peter stood up with the Eleven, raised his voice, and addressed the crowd: 'Fellow Jews and all of you who live in Jerusalem, let me explain this to you; listen carefully to what I say. These people are not drunk, as you suppose. It's only nine in the morning! No, this is what was spoken by the prophet Joel: "In the last days, God says, I will pour out my Spirit on all people. Your sons and daughters will prophesy, your young men will see visions, your old men will dream dreams. Even on my servants, both men and women, I will pour out my Spirit in those days, and they will prophesy."'

We stand at a spiritually strategic period in time. It is a God-appointed time on the loom of eternity. The Divine Weaver is actively threading past experiences with future purposes, and the invitation is for every believer to move from being a loose, unattached thread to an important part of a glorious, clear tapestry of global impact. This is not a call to ordinary activity, but to a divine awakening: a thoughtful spiritual quickening from deep sleep of ineffectiveness into the resurrection power of the Holy Spirit. It is a call from the Spirit of God to the spirits of believers for spiritual mobilization and alignment, positioning believers for divine engagement and unprecedented expansion of the Kingdom of God.

This call reveals the meaning of the example set forth in Acts 2, demonstrating that Pentecost was not a one-time event but the sample for a continually available dimension of Spirit-empowered life intended to mobilize the entire Body of Christ. From inactivity to potential power in progress: The activating of a Divine Awakening (Acts 2:1-13). Before Peter could preach the sermon in our focal text, there had to be an awakening. The 120 in the Upper Room transitioned from a state of waiting (a purposeful inactivity) to a state of overwhelming encounter. This shift is critical. The Greek word for "wind" (anemos) in Acts 2:2 is "breath." It goes back to Ezekiel's vision of the valley of dry bones (Ezekiel 37:9-10), where breath (wind and spirit) transformed a scattered, lifeless army into a mobilized, living, and powerful force.

This was not a gentle breeze, but a violent, rushing wind, a symbol of God's disruptive power to awaken what is not active. The "tongues of fire" (v. 3) signify purification, empowerment, and divine authorization. The fire did not merely warm them; it rested upon each one of them. This is a deeply personal and empowering act of the Spirit, not for the spiritual renown, but for every believer, men, women, young, and old. The initial evidence was their speaking in "other tongues" (v. 4), a miraculous sign of a reversal of the Tower of Babel, where human confusion is now overcome by divine communication for global gospel impact. The awakening, therefore, is twofold: (1) Internal: The infilling of the Holy Spirit (the breath of God). (2) External: The empowerment for cross-cultural, effective witness (the fire of God). This move from inactivity to dynamism is the first step off the bench and onto the loom.

Peter, freshly empowered, rises to interpret the event not simply as a new practice but as the fulfillment of prophecy. His quote of Joel 2:28-32 is the Spirit's heart of the message and the blueprint for spiritual mobilization. Peter introduces the quote with a powerful phrase: "In the last days…" This is not a distant, future period, but the mark of a new spiritual season, the season of the Messiah, the time between Pentecost and the abiding presence, the return of Jesus.

We are living in the "last days," meaning this prophecy is currently active and operational. This mobilization being described eliminates every human ladder and barrier: "I will pour out my Spirit on all people." (v. 17): The Greek word (ekcheō) used here means "to pour out generously and impressively, to shed forth." This is an abundant, unselective outpouring. The barrier between spiritual leaders and the congregation is demolished. The Spirit is no longer reserved for prophets, priests, and kings but for all flesh. "Your sons and daughters will prophesy." (v. 17): Gender is rendered irrelevant in the Spirit's distribution of gifts. Daughters are mobilized alongside sons.

"Young men… old men…" (v. 17): Ministry based on age is abolished. The potential of youth and the wisdom of age are both sanctified and activated by the same Spirit. "Even on my servants, both men and women." (v. 18): The Greek word for servants here means bondservants, those of the lowest social rank. The class system is overturned. The Spirit mobilizes from the bottom up. This is the divine design for the Church, a fully mobilized, spirit-filled movement of empowered witnesses. The supernatural gifts of the Spirit (prophecy, visions, dreams) are not optional or extras but the critical equipment for this mobilization. They provide the spiritual gifts and insights (dreams and visions) and the timely, divine communication (prophecy) needed for effective engagement and expansion in a dark world. A church that neglects this broad-range mobilization is operating at a fraction of its God-intended capacity.

The Power of Alignment

Acts 2:42-47

An awakened and mobilized collection of threads is not yet a tapestry until it is aligned. There has to be the weaving of threads into alignment. Without alignment, there is only disorder. Alignment is the process by which individual believers, in their awakened state, yield to the Master Weaver's hand to be placed in right relationship with God, with one another, and with the purpose of His mission. The power of alignment is seen in the immediate results of Acts 2:42-47.

There are five basic alignments necessary to be God's tapestry of impact: (1) Alignment of Doctrine: *"They devoted themselves to the apostles' teaching…" (v. 42*). They aligned their beliefs with apostolic truth. (2) Alignment of Relationship: "*…and to fellowship…"* (v. 42). They aligned their lives in community, breaking down individual independence. (3) Alignment in Holy Communion: "…to the breaking of bread and to prayer." (v. 42). They aligned their worship vertically with God. It is to align the spirit, soul, and body to Jesus. In partaking of the Holy Communion, a believer unites and consecrates their life to a covenant with Jesus through baptism, in life, death, and resurrection. (4) Economic Alignment: "They sold property and possessions to give to anyone who had need." (v. 45). They aligned their resources with the Kingdom's priorities. (5) Alignment in Evangelism: "And the Lord added to their number daily those who were being saved." (v. 47). It is alignment with the body of Jesus in witnessing, outreach, and soul winning. The natural result of this alignment was explosive expansion.

Alignment is a work of the Holy Spirit. It is He who confers unity (1 Corinthians 12:13) and distributes gifts "as he determines" (1 Corinthians 12:11). A believer's role is to surrender in obedience. It allows a believer to be woven into the pattern that the Holy Spirit has designed, even when the believer cannot see the whole picture from their limited, "thread's-eye" view. A single thread has little strength and limited impact. But woven together with many others, it becomes part of an exponential result "…And the Lord added to the Church daily such as to be saved" (v. 47b). This is a Tapestry of Impact that displays the gifts, wisdom, and glory of God in oneness (Ephesians 3:10). A believer's testimony, empowered by the Spirit and aligned in community, becomes part of an outstanding narrative of salvation and transformation that stretches across generations and cultures.

Alignment is a critical and urgent call of the divine loom. The sound of the rushing wind is still clear and distinct. The fire of God is still available to rest upon every believer. The prophecy of Joel is still in effect. The Divine Loom is active, and the Kairos moment is now. This call is to:

(1) Arise from sleep and be convicted of spiritual complacency, ineffectiveness, and self-reliance. Cry out for a fresh, personal fire baptism, a Divine Awakening that fills a believer with the breath and fire of the Holy Spirit. (2) Embrace full mobilization and step into the Spirit-empowered identity in Jesus. Whether the believer is a son or daughter, young or old, they are called and authorized to operate in the supernatural gifts of the

Spirit for the sake of the unsaved world. (3) Submit to spiritual Alignment by yielding to the Master Weaver. Commit to the apostolic teaching, deep fellowship, sacrificial worship, and radical generosity that position the entire Body of Christ for maximum impact.

Do not remain a disconnected thread. Allow the Holy Spirit to awaken, mobilize, and align you, for it is only on the Loom of Eternity that our individual lives are woven into the magnificent, world-altering Tapestry of Impact, from thread to testimony, for the glory of God and the expansion of his Kingdom. The Spirit is speaking to the Body of Christ, "Arise, shine, for your light has come, and the glory of the Lord rises upon you" (Isaiah 60:1). Let the church awake and be woven in line with God's tapestry.

> *"For our light affliction, which is but for a moment, works for us a far more exceeding and eternal weight of glory."*

The word "tapestry" is gotten from the Old French word "tapisserie," which is from the Latin word "tapes," that means "cloth" or "woven fabric." A tapestry is a work of intricate design, where vertical threads and horizontal threads are interlaced into a single masterpiece. The vertical threads provide tension and strength from top to bottom; the horizontal threads create weaves on the underside, the over-side, and around the vertical threads, which form the pattern. This interplay symbolizes unity, structure, and storylines that lead to the ultimate goal of a classical masterpiece.

"Glory" in the Hebrew and Greek languages carries the idea of weight, honor, wonder, and divine illumination. When joined, "The Tapestry of Glory" unveils the divine account of

God weaving His eternal weight of glory into the Church and the life of the believer. Each trial is a thread. What looks like tangled knots on the underside is, from heaven's side, the woven pattern of eternal glory. Glory is not only God's presence and brightness, but His manifested purpose in His people, woven into times, past, present, and future (Romans 8:18-19). God weaves His glory into dwelling places: tabernacle, temple, and now believers and the Church (Exodus 40:34-35; 1 Cor. 6:19). In Christ, the tapestry is complete, God is interwoven with, in, and through man (John 1:14). Each believer is a thread, chosen and dyed in Jesus' blood through the Holy Spirit, carrying the unique colors of calling and grace. Calling is the believer's guaranteed assurance of endurance in a race between light and darkness. Grace is the believer's shield, shelter, and fortress that brings out their sacrifice of worship and praise. The vertical thread represents God's unchanging covenant promises. His Word stretched from the believer's past (beginning) to the believer's future (end). The horizontal thread is the spirit's movements through time, weaving each moment into alignment with the eternal purpose. Jesus is the pattern, the central person and idea, into whose image believers are woven (Romans 8:29). What appears chaotic on earth is the unfinished underside of the divine tapestry. But on the contrary, prophetically, heaven sees the masterpiece, the Tapestry of Glory.

Every believer bears a sacred or spiritually concealed importance. The Spirit clothes them not in weak fabric but as glory-loaded threads within the tapestry (Isaiah 61:10). The tapestry is never stationary in its revelation. It grows, deepens, and is becoming more radiant (2 Corinthians 3:18). Threads alone cannot form beauty; only when interwoven do they reveal the pattern. Likewise, the Body of Christ reveals God's glory corporately (Ephesians 4:16). The Spiritual Fathers of the Faith spoke of "theosis," the participation of believers in divine nature and glory. Augustine, one of the most important Church fathers, called the believer's journey "a weaving together of grace and response." Believers who sought God during the middle ages likened his wisdom to the art of decorating fabric, knots of suffering on one side, but beauty revealed on the other. To the spirit-filled believers, glory is not only a future destiny but a present experience. It is manifested in salvation, healings, deliverance, miracles, prophetic utterances, and corporate worship as a sample of the eternal pattern that lies ahead. Moses' Face (Exodus 34:29–35), his facial appearance, became part of the tapestry, shining with reflected glory. The Early Church (Acts 2) was a diverse community of people from various backgrounds and gifts, all united by the Spirit in a single fabric.

Intercession is aligning believers' prayers with the Weaver's mind, pulling threads of promise into manifestation through faith. Prophecy is seeing the pattern before it becomes fully apparent. Worship is the loom on which threads of heaven and earth interlace, creating a space where glory reigns. Prophetically, The Tapestry of Glory is not just history but destiny, a vision of believers and the Church colorfully and brightly, woven into Christ, displaying "the manifold wisdom of God" (Ephesians 3:10). The Tapestry of Glory is God's eternal masterpiece: woven from covenant threads, dyed in Christ's blood, stretched on the cross of the loom, and patterned with the destiny of the believers. What others see as brokenness, God calls beauty; what some perceive as delay, God calls design. The prophetic call is to trust the Weaver, yield as threads, and behold the emerging glory of His tapestry on display.

> *"For the earth will be filled with the knowledge of the glory of the LORD, as the waters cover the sea"* ***(Habakkuk 2:14).***

The Tapestry of Glory

Esther 4:14-16

> *"And who knows whether you have not come to the kingdom for such a time as this?" (Esther 4:14 (ESV))*

Esther is introduced in Scripture as a young Jewish woman living in exile in Persia during the reign of King Ahasuerus (Xerxes I). She was originally named Hadassah, but was known as Esther (Esther 2:7). Orphaned at a young age, she was raised by her cousin Mordecai, who played a significant role in her life and calling.

When King Ahasuerus removed Queen Vashti from her position (Esther 1:10–22), a search began for a new queen. Esther was taken into the king's court and, through God's favor, was chosen above all others to become queen (Esther 2:17). Though elevated to royalty, she kept her Jewish identity hidden at Mordecai's instruction (Esther 2:10).

The turning point of her story comes when Haman, a high-ranking official, plots to destroy all the Jews in the Persian Empire (Esther 3:5–6). Mordecai urges Esther to intercede with the king, reminding her that she may have been placed in her royal position *"for such a time as this"* (Esther 4:14). Though approaching the king without invitation could cost her life

(Esther 4:11), Esther chooses courage over fear and declares, *"If I perish, I perish"* (Esther 4:16). Esther exposes Haman's plot during a banquet (Esther 7:1–6), leading to Haman's downfall (Esther 7:9–10) and the deliverance of the Jewish people (Esther 8:11–17).

The life of Esther in scripture reveals a spiritual truth that appears negative from the beginning. And then, at the conclusion, it brought forth a hidden spiritual reality that the natural mind finds difficult to understand. God's name is never mentioned in the story of Esther, yet his invisible presence is clearly interwoven throughout her story. From a spiritual perspective, Esther's story reveals how the Holy Spirit operates even when unseen and unmentioned. He works destiny through divine timing, prophetic positioning, and invisible influence. Esther's story is an art in God's tapestry of the hidden thread in divine glory. Jesus was God hiding in man for divine glory. It is courage, timing, and divine intervention that reveal that what is hidden in the Spirit becomes visible in glory. Esther's account is a testimony to the mysterious ways of the Spirit (John 3:8). Though the Spirit isn't named, His invisible hand is evident in weaving every thread of Esther's journey. Romans 8:28 says, "All things work together for good..." Proverbs 21:1 also says, "The king's heart is in the hand of the Lord..."

Believers don't always feel the presence of the Holy Spirit, but that doesn't mean the anointing isn't upon them and working. Esther 4:14 is a divine moment when the Spirit of God intercepted a satanic destiny planned for the people of God. It was when a divine moment collided with a man's intended moment. It was also where believers' destiny intersected with God's purpose. It was where Chronos, man's time, intersected with Kairos, God's moment. It was a Spirit-ordained timing and divine opportunity, and Esther had no idea.

"For such a time as this…" is a phrase that awakened a prophetic activation. The Spirit was summoning Esther to step into alignment with heaven's calendar. Example: Like David facing Goliath or Mary agreeing to carry Jesus. It was a "spiritual tipping point moment" in Esther's life. Every believer faces "spiritual tipping point moments" in their life. It is a moment that calls for the choice of unshakable hope. The three Hebrew boys believed in God and hoped against hope in a fiery furnace moment in a furnace that was seven times hotter than any hot fire. Daniel hoped against hope, believing in God in the den of lions. For Esther, it caused a silence that could have been considered a spiritual disobedience. There are moments in the life of a believer when silence is equal to disagreement with the Holy Spirit and alignment with darkness. With God, every moment with Him is a window of spiritual opportunity for a believer. Ezekiel 3:18 let believers know that failure to adhere to the Holy Spirit's guidance and direction can result to serious spiritual consequences. For the Prophet Ezekiel, it was to warn others of an impending spiritual danger. Such moments bring about spiritual accountability for the believer. Silence can grieve the Spirit (Eph. 4:30).

"…relief and deliverance will rise for the Jews from another place…"

This acknowledges God's sovereignty. He has multiple possibilities, but obedience brings a believer into divine alignment and favor. Like Elijah, who thought he was the only prophet left, but God had Elisha and others hidden in the wings

(1 Kings 19:18).

"…but you and your father's house will perish" (Esther 4:14). This verse is a stark reminder that failure to act in faith towards God can cost a believer their legacy in Christ.

"And who knows whether you have not come to the kingdom for such a time as this?"

This is the climactic invitation, a moment dependent on a favorable response to stepping into a Spirit-led destiny. Not fate, but faith in divine orchestration. Esther didn't just fall into purpose; she was positioned and provoked into it. A spirit-filled believer should understand that inactivity is the enemy of their calling. *2 Tim. 1:6 – "Fan into flame the gift of God…"*

There was a woman of God in ministry who felt left out and passed over. But in a moment of God's choice and timing, she was elevated and placed into the spotlight, not by desire, but by obedience, faith, and a prophetic calling. Esther was not called to enjoy comfort; she was placed there to be an intercessor and deliverer. Luke 4:18 says, "The Spirit of the Lord is upon me, because He has anointed me…" The anointing of God isn't a decoration to wear and bluff, it is for service and sacrifice for God.

Intercession unlocks divine outcomes. Esther's first move wasn't political; it was spiritual. "Go, gather all the Jews… and fast for me…" (Esther 4:16). This calls for the believer's reliance on prayer, fasting, and prophetic action before breakthrough. Esther's thread in God's tapestry turned from hidden obedience to public deliverance. Haman, the agent of Satan who wanted to cause an extinction of God's people was exposed and destroyed (Esther 7); The enemy's hand turned the heart of Haman to turn the heart of the King, but God's hand had turned king's heart towards Esther through intercessory fast and prayer (Esther 6); The people were saved (Esther 8); "Purim," a Jewish day of celebration is established as a celebration of reversal and redemption What is done in the secret place becomes visible in the glory of open testimony (Matt. 6:6, Ps. 91:1). Believers are part of God's divine tapestry, woven with intention, hidden for a season, and called into visibility. Like Esther, a believer's life may feel ordinary, silent, or unseen, but the Holy Spirit is always at work behind the veil. He is also weaving purpose in each moment of a believer's life. Step forward, even if your knees shake. Intercede even if others remain silent. Obey even when it costs your comfort. Trust the hidden thread of the threads in the Tapestry of the Spirit. "And who knows if YOU have come to the kingdom… for such a time as this?"

Chapter 7

The Spiritual Chemistry Through a Divine Tapestry

John 17:10-11, 17; 1 Cor. 3:9, 12; 1 Pet. 2:5

Chemistry is the science that deals with the identification of an object, its properties, composition, structure, and how it changes, operates, or is transformed. God's intention in making man from an object of mud and clay was to cause a spiritual reaction in man, by the breath of His Spirit, that would transform man into God Himself. It was for man to be transformed into a unique being, to be very precious, as implied by the figures of gold, bdellium (pearls), and precious stones (Ezekiel 28:13-15; 2 Cor. 3:17-18; Gen. 2:11-12). According to these Scriptures, God is seeking men of clay to be transformed into his image, that is, transformed into believers who, through faith, will be precious to Him, and be built together as a living organism into the Body of Christ (1 Cor. 3:9, 12; 1 Pet. 2:5; Eph. 4:16).

In chemistry, transformation occurs through the reaction of two chemicals combining to form a single compound. If we want to cause an object to be transformed into something else, we must blend or graft another thing into it. Only when some other matter is mixed into the cup does the original chemical matter begin to be transformed. For instance, when sodium and chloride are mixed in a container, they form table salt. Man, an object of clay was to be transformed, by a spiritual infusion with God's Spirit, into a product compare to gold, pearls, and precious stones. 2 Corinthians 3:18 says, "We all with unveiled face, beholding and reflecting like a mirror the glory of the Lord, are being transformed into the same image from glory to glory, even as from the Lord Spirit."

Spiritually, as men of clay, we were brought to life through contact with the breath of God. Through Adam, all men bear a fallen nature. Like chemical matters, they need to be transformed by union. So, through a spiritual union, the spiritual gifts and nature in Jesus transformed the nature of the natural man, made of mud and clay, into the nature and gifts of God. For a natural person to be transformed, they must be reborn in Christ, the spiritual incubator. When a person accepts Jesus as Lord and Savior, a new creation of that person comes into existence. Christ was infused into that person's spirit; a spiritual reaction took place within that person in the same way that a chemical reaction takes place. Something divine, heavenly, and spiritual was added to that person; they became a believer. By being mingled and blended with Christ in regeneration, believers were transformed from men of clay into men of gold, pearl, and precious stones, vessels for God's glory. This is a wonderful, divine, and glorious formation of a divine tapestry. Each thread of a man is dyed in the blood of Jesus, gifted with the unique qualities of God, empowered by the Holy Spirit, positioned in Christ, and placed in the Body of Christ for divine purpose and assignment.

The Spiritual Chemistry of a believer in Christ is spiritual regeneration. It is the renewal of the soul of a believer, through a spiritual chain reaction caused by union with the grace of Jesus Christ. It is a change conducted by the Holy Spirit that transforms a believer from a state of fleshliness, characterized by spiritual dryness and unavailability, into a new creation in Christ. It is the regeneration of a person, with a new spiritual structure, new spiritual properties, and an eternal destiny. Such a believer undergoes a continuous process of sanctification until they reach their final, stable state of perfection in glory. Salvation is a one-time event that involves a continuous process of justification through the blood and grace of Jesus. It initiates an eternal process of purification known as sanctification. This is like a continuous separation or refinement from sin. It is a process where the Holy Spirit, through the "heat" of life's circumstances that cause sin, and the solution of Jesus to dissolve or automatically remove it. God's Word gradually removes impurities (sinful habits and patterns) to produce sanctification and concentration of Christlike properties in the believer.

Transformation is the heart of spiritual chemistry, the process of change. It releases the awesome power of the resurrection of Christ and grace into the life of the believer. This is from the reaction of substitution caused by salvation. Christ takes our sin, we take His righteousness (2 Corinthians 5:21).

The Holy Spirit then becomes the witness, enforcer, and empowerment of this new union. He facilitates this reaction in Dunamis fashion without the believer being consumed by it. The Holy Spirit convicts and initiates this reaction process by revealing sin, erasing it, providing the necessary needs, and empowering the believer, all at the same time. The Law acts as a spiritual agent that reveals sin and sounds the alarm for the need for a spiritual reaction, but cannot enable it. It exposes sin but can't remove it. Jesus' perfect life, sacrificial death, and resurrection provide the necessary elements for the reaction: righteousness, atonement, and life. The Grace of God through Jesus Christ is the divine element that seals the new change from the spiritual reaction. This is the power of the Blood and the Cross!

***

Esther 4:14-16

The book of Esther demonstrates a strange realization. God is never mentioned personally, yet his vision saturates every detail. Vision, spiritually in this passage, is not merely foresight, it is the unveiling of God's divine plan (Proverbs 29:18). Mordecai discerned that Esther's position was not accidental but God-given: "And who knows whether you have not come to the kingdom for such a time as this?" (Esther 4:14). The lifting or unfolding of vision here was not Esther's personal desire but a divine shift in pattern, moving her from palace beauty to prophetic intercessor. When vision rises, it becomes clear, and it then creates the atmosphere for power to be shifted. Esther's elevated discernment became the driving force that destabilized Haman's evil decree and repositioned the throne of Persia under divine alignment and in favor of the Jews. Every paradigm shift in Scripture precedes a fresh outpouring of anointing. Joseph's shift from prison to palace released him into governing wisdom (Genesis. 41). David's shift from shepherd to giant-slayer launched him toward kingship (1 Samuel 17). Similarly, Esther's shift from silent queen to bold advocate released a mantle of authority that shook the Persian empire and literally placed the King's scepter in Esther's favor. Her ordeal reflects the spiritual principle that the fast she and her people engaged in (Esther 4:16) was not simply a preparation for persuading the King, but a shift in their spiritual position. Fasting aligned her with divine power, elevating her anointing for intercession. This confirms the spiritual truth that when God disrupts a believer's comfort zones, he releases the power of grace for kingdom advancement.

Esther's vision was born out of a spiritual struggle. Before approaching the king, she said, *"If I perish, I perish"* (Esther 4:16). This intercessory obedience became the point at which things began to turn. Vision without intercession is powerless; intercession without vision is aimless. When both came together in Esther, the throne shifted, and the king extended his golden scepter (Esth. 5:2). This moment was more than royal favor; it was divine elevation. Spiritually, it mirrors the principle of Isaiah 6:1, where *"in the year King Uzziah died, I saw the Lord sitting on a throne, high and lifted up."* Control of powers turns when vision aligns with the Spirit's call to pray. The spiritual wonder here reveals that the shifting of patterns by the Kingdom of God is a disruption of purpose and intent by the Spirit in the kingdom of the earth. It is not just a matter of circumstances but of discernment. When God lifts a vision, it's because a throne or control of power is about to shift, and the mission is about to race forward. In the Book of Esther, a mystery is revealed. God, who was unnoticed, was evidently present. His sovereignty orchestrated a significant shift from a demonic political ambition to prophetic and spiritual dimensions.

This is not just a historic moment; it's a spirit revelation. When Heaven's vision arises, earthly thrones rearrange, and God's mission accelerates. The lives of Esther and Mordecai reveal how divine disruption can create an elevated anointing and accelerate destiny. God's pattern shifts come first before power shifts. Moses sees the burning bush, Pharaoh's dominion is shaken, and Israel begins her exodus; Isaiah sees the Lord (Isaiah 6) King Uzziah dies and Isaiah is sent as a prophet; Paul is blinded by glory, religious structures is challenged, and the Gospel begins to invade the gentile world; John sees the throne (Revelation 4), Heaven's judgments is activated, and the church receives the end-times revelation and mandate. Esther hears Mordecai's cry and receives the revelation to fast and pray; Haman's system and plan are dismantled, and Israel's deliverance is set in motion and accelerated. Mordecai represents the prophetic move, those who see what the Spirit is doing and call others into alignment. He discerns the enemy's plot (Esther 4:1); He provokes Esther into purpose (Esther 4:14), and He declares divine consequence or elevation depending on obedience. Mordecai's insight is what activates the pattern shift in Esther's mind. Without it, anointing remains dormant. *"If I perish, I perish"* (Esther 4:16). This statement is more than bravery. It is the death of a false pattern, the surrendering of personal defense in exchange for divine purpose. It is at this moment that Esther transitions from a queen of beauty to a warrior intercessor, from royal procedure to divine petition, from a survival mindset to a sacrificial mantle. The spiritual truth here is that the Spirit anoints a believer AFTER they surrender their system and agenda.

Divine Disruption Releases Supernatural Elevation

Esther 4:13-17

And Mordecai told them to answer Esther: "Do not think in your heart that you will escape in the king's palace any more than all the other Jews. 14) For if you remain completely silent at this time, relief and deliverance will arise for the Jews from another place, but you and your father's house will perish. Yet who knows whether you have come to the kingdom for such a time as this?"

15) Then Esther told them to reply to Mordecai: 16) "Go, gather all the Jews who are present in Shushan, and fast for me; neither eat nor drink for three days, night or day. My maids and I will fast likewise. And so I will go to the king, which is against the law; and if I perish, I perish!"

17)So Mordecai went his way and did according to all that Esther commanded him.

From a Spirit-empowered viewpoint, Esther's story is not just a tale of the past, but a prophetic pattern. God allows disruption to pull apart human systems so that his Kingdom's order can be obvious. The plan and device that Haman developed for hanging became the means of his downfall, while Mordecai and Esther were elevated to positions of extraordinary influence. This spiritual principle is evident throughout the Bible. Example: The "infilling" or "baptism of the Holy Spirit," in the Upper Room, was a disruption of Jewish tradition. It opened up to the believers and the Church the evidence of the Holy Spirit and an unfamiliar, yet elevated anointing (Acts 2). Saul's persecution disrupted the early believers, yet it caused the gospel to be scattered throughout the earth (Acts 8:4). When vision lifts, when God gives a people divine insight, thrones, systems, and powers will be shifted to make room and welcome His sovereign design. Vision comes ahead of spiritual elevation. Ministries that walk in divine revelation and spiritual insight experience divine shifts. A Paradigm shift is usually before the fresh oil of anointing. The anointing is not stationary; it flows and increases as believers become sensitive to and embrace divine disruption. Divine disruption is not destruction but spiritual preparation. God shakes the systems of men to establish Jesus' agendas (Hebrews 12:27-28). Prayers and Intercession together form the bridge to deliverance and breakthrough. Like Esther, the Church must labor in prayers and intercessions before experiencing the Throne Room. The anointing follows divine alignment. When God finds a vessel who aligns vision with spiritual surrender through prayer and intercession, thrones shift and mantles drop and increase on the lives of believers and ministries.

The rise of Haman's satanic-influence movement raises the faith of Esther to receive the King's scepter, and reopen the closed book of Mordecai's heroic deed done on behalf of the King. Remembrance also brought about a paradigm shift, revealing what happens when vision lifts and thrones shift. Haman symbolizes the exaltation of the flesh and of human systems that oppose God's covenant people. Scripture says: "After these things King Ahasuerus promoted Haman … and advanced him, and set his seat above all the princes that were with him" (Esther 3:1). The power that Haman sought was based on politics, not divine purpose. His authority was driven by pride, punishment, and a demonic agenda, seeking to completely wipe out God's covenant people. His decree of death represented the counterfeit throne of the adversary, always seeking to silence God's vision-bearers. Yet, in divine mystery, God often allows the counterfeit to rise first so that His dominion may be revealed when He overturns it (Psalm 37:35–36). When Esther appeared uninvited before the king, she

risked death (Esther 4:11). Yet, through prayer and intercession, the king favored Esther and extended to her his scepter of gold (Esther 5:2). In those days, a scepter was an ultimate symbol of royalty of the king that symbolized the king's power and rule. It represented both authority and favor (Psalm 45:6; Hebrews 1:8). This was the critical moment of power shifting. The shame and weakness of Esther's hidden Jewish identity, Hadassah (meaning "Myrtle"), now served as her divine assignment as a deliverer. The extension of King's scepter was a spiritual indication. The collision of Heaven's vision with fleshly authorities was taking place. Where Haman sought destruction, God released His keeping power through Esther's faith and obedience. Here, we see that when vision was lifted in the Spirit (through Esther's intercession and fasting), the throne shifted in the natural.
The final turn came when the king's sleepless night led to the reading of the chronicles (Esther 6:1-3). The remembrance of Mordecai's earlier act of loyalty became the divine hinge-point: The king asked, "What honor or dignity has been bestowed on Mordecai for this?" (Esther 6:3).

Haman, who had plotted Mordecai's death, was commanded to clothe him in royal robes and lead him on the king's horse (Esther 6:10-11). This prophetic reversal reveals that God can use the enemy to exalt his chosen vessels. The remembrance of Mordecai was not an occurrence that happened by mistake, but a matter of divine timing. When God's vision is embraced, his scepter is extended, and He also remembers and rewards covenant faithfulness. Haman's rise showed the weak exaltation of the flesh. The King's scepter extended to Esther reveals the divine favor that comes through vision, intercession, and obedience. Mordecai's remembrance was a prophetic principle of Psalm 75:6-7: *"For promotion cometh neither from the east, nor from the west, nor from the south. But God is the judge: He putteth down one, and setteteh up another."* This tapestry of patterns' shift teaches believers that when God disrupts a human pattern, He not only stops the rise of the system of the enemy but also exalts the humble believer who has remained faithful. Every Haman in ministry (false systems, pride, opposition) will rise only to be overthrown by God's ultimate power. Every Esther (intercessor with divine vision) who risks surrender will see the scepter of divine favor extended. Every Mordecai (faithful servant) will be remembered and lifted, even when overlooked for a season. The Spirit-filled principle here is that pattern shifts may occur through evil disruption, but they end in elevation when a divine shift restores them.

Chapter 8

Psalm 23: The WrinkleFree Soul

Psalm 23

The Lord is my shepherd; I shall not want. 2 He makes me to lie down in [b]green pastures;

He leads me beside the [c]still waters. 3 He restores my soul; He leads me in the paths of righteousness For His name's sake. 4 Yea, though I walk through the valley of the shadow of death, I will fear no evil; For You are with me; Your rod and Your staff, they comfort me.

5 You prepare a table before me in the presence of my enemies; You anoint my head with oil;

My cup runs over. 6 Surely goodness and mercy shall follow me All the days of my life; And I will dwell in the house of the Lord Forever.

"...He restoreth my soul: He leadeth me in the path of righteousness for His name's sake..." (Psalm 23:3)

Imagine for a moment a fabric that defies wrinkles! A fabric that, though folded, pressed, or trapped beneath the weight of countless other materials, yet it rises to normal. It returns to its original state, its properties restore themselves, it smooths out, not by ironing, not by external heat, but by design from a Divine reactant. A reactant is the primary substance in a chemical reaction that is responsible for the transformation of another substance into a completely new product. A transformation of such nature is physically abnormal but spiritually normal. It is a product of excellence, a divine creativity of a Master craftsman. Such fabric is a wrinkle-free fabric, but not the kind stitched in earthly factories. This is heaven's cloth, woven in redemption, dyed in the blood of Christ, sealed by the spirit, and crafted in the eternal loom. It is a fabric uniquely designed by God in His own chemistry lab, through His divine imagination. Just like this unique fabric, the believer, though burdened. Though pressed by life, though appearing crushed, is never truly wrinkled. Why? Because the believer has been recreated in spirit and is being daily restored in the soul by the renewing power of the Word of God and the Holy Spirit.

A believer battling terminal illness sounded very confused when asked whether they were afraid of death. The believer said, "I shouldn't be, but somehow I am." When asked why? They replied, I am not afraid of dying, because I know that everyone will have to face death someday. What I am fearful of is facing the father's judgment. There are some dark areas of my soul after I was born again. I have prayed, fasted, and repented several times, yet there is no peace in my soul. And I am not sure if I am included in the redeemed." Then, a spirit-filled believer standing close by said, "The soul of a believer was not designed to be comforted by emotions; it is designed to be restored by the word through the renewing of the believer's mind by the Word of God."

It is mind-blowing to try to tie together the visual image of a "wrinkle-free fabric" with the believer's identity, restoration, and divine design in Jesus. In a perfect description by the Holy Spirit, David captured the spiritual concept of God's eternal plan for the soul of a believer in Psalm 23. He painted a clear picture of the divine security of the believer's soul that is distinct and vastly different from the soul of an unbeliever. In nature, a wrinkle-free fabric is crafted with delicate and careful attention. No matter how crumpled, folded, or compressed between layers, given a bit of time, sometimes overnight, it returns to its smooth, elegant form without human effort. This is because the fibers or threads of the fabric were engineered to remember and return to their original state. In the spiritual realm, the believer's soul reflects this reality (Romans 12:2). The Master Weaver weaves believers with threads that are self-restorative and cannot be broken. They are the threads of redemption (forgiveness, deliverance, and restoration), grace, and glory. These threads are also interwoven into patterns that are beautiful, amazing, and mysterious. They are designed to withstand the squeezes, pressures, and dark storage spaces of life ("the valley of the shadow of death").

***Psalm 23:3** says, "He restores my soul."* Salvation is not a clearance bargain of unwanted goods on the rack of eternity waiting to be auctioned to free up space. It is God's Masterpiece.

God Himself has woven and clothed a believer's soul through the spiritual chemistry. A spiritual chemistry of a recreated spirit called "regeneration." This is done by His righteousness, designing the believer for Divine presentation before Heaven and earth (Psalm 23:3b). – "…He leads me in the 'path of righteousness for His name's sake'…" Believers are set on the path of righteousness with Jesus' name at stake. A wrinkle-free fabric is not made by accident; it is an infusion of loom, thread, and tapestry with intentionality. Likewise, the believer's salvation was crafted in the eternal counsel of God before the foundations of the world.

Ephesians 2:10: *"For we are His workmanship, created in Christ Jesus for good works, which God prepared beforehand that we should walk in them."*

For a believer to be spiritually contaminated and condemned is for Jesus to fail in His craftsmanship of the believers' souls. Isaiah 61:10 says, "He has clothed me with the garments of salvation, He has covered me with the robe of righteousness." Restoration of the soul of a believer is "built in." There is an automatic soul renewal in every true believer. A wrinkle-free garment retains its smooth form due to the way the fibers of the cloth were treated and set. In the same way, a believer's soul remembers its re-created position of perfection in Christ. 2 Corinthians 5:17 says, "If anyone is in Christ, he is a new creation; old things have passed away; behold, all things have become new." Romans 12:2 says, "Be transformed by the renewing of your mind." Psalm 103:2-3 says, "Bless the Lord, O my soul, and forget not all His benefits: who forgives all your iniquities; who heals all your diseases." Paul made this prophetic statement of promise, Ephesians 5:25-27: "…Just as Christ loved the church and gave Himself up for her 26 to sanctify her, cleansing her by the washing with water through the word, 27 and to present her to Himself as a glorious church, without stain or wrinkle or any such blemish, but holy and blameless."

Psalm 23:3

"He restores my soul; He leads me in the paths of righteousness For His name's sake"

Proverbs 24:10

"If you faint in the day of adversity, your strength is small."

The life of God within you is not fragile; it is resilient. Your spirit is recreated instantly at salvation, and your soul is restored progressively as you meditate on the Word of God. Proverbs 24:10, in garment terms, this is like a fabric that collapses under pressure, revealing it was poorly made. But the child of God is no "poor specimen." When the believer is crushed, folded by life's disappointments, or weighed down by the heavy burden of spiritual battle, the word of God acts like the warm breath of the Spirit that restores the soul's shape. A wrinkle-free garment has tensile strength, the ability to stretch without tearing, and rebound without losing its form. Spiritually, the stress-withstanding strength of the believer comes from: (1) The Word of God, feeding daily on scripture. (2) The Spirit of God, dwelling consciously in His presence. (3) The armor of God – standing firm in warfare. When the believer is squeezed by trials, the Spirit within pushes back and restores their outlook and expression, courage, and confidence in Christ.

A wrinkle-free garment is made to be worn with confidence, ready for display at any moment without last-minute repairs. Likewise, the believer's life is designed for presentation before kings, nations, and most importantly, before God, angels, and the cloud of witnesses (Hebrews 12:1-2). A presentation never complains before its presenter. Ephesians 5:27 says, "That He might present her to Himself a glorious church, not having spot or wrinkle or any such thing, but that she should be holy and without blemish." This is not only about ethical perfection, but spiritual readiness; it is about the believer being ready for God's assignment at any moment, with no delay or need for spiritual ironing. A life in the Spirit is "wrinkle-free" not because it never gets ruffled by trouble, but because it is pre-treated with the oil of joy, the balm of grace, and the fire of the Spirit. From a Spirit-filled perspective, this truth calls believers into "faith rest:" When the world folds a believer up, they should "Worship" until God's presence releases the wrinkles; When trials press against a child of God, they should "Speak" the Rhema Word until hope stretches out again; When offenses stain a saint of God, they should "Allow" forgiveness to flow until purity shines once more. In the spirit-filled life, believers don't just hope for restoration; they expect it. Christians are predestined to be restored. The Holy Spirit within is the built-in wrinkle-release feature of the Kingdom garment.

The wonders of a quality wrinkle-free fabric remind believers that their life in Christ is not fragile but resilient, not temporary but eternal. The believer is crafted, restored, and displayed by the Master Weaver Himself. Salvation is not cheap; it is a priceless, Spirit-woven garment that remembers eternity even when temporarily crushed by time. "He restores my soul." And when the Master is finished, the wrinkles will be no more. The Master Weaver didn't create this indestructible, self-restoring fabric to remain crumpled in a drawer! "You are a chosen generation, a royal priesthood, a holy nation, His own special people, that you may proclaim the praises of Him who called you out of darkness into His marvelous light!" (1 Peter 2:9). Believers are designed for spiritual and worldly presentations! To reflect His glory! To showcase the wonders of His restorative grace! When the world sees a soul, seemingly crushed by circumstances, rise again, not by its own power, but by the automatic, inborn power of Christ within, that is a testimony that shakes the gates of hell! We are positioned to present the living Christ!

The Eternal Fabric of the Soul

Psalm 23:3; Proverbs 24:10

Understanding the truth behind a mystery woven not by human hands, but by the Master Designer himself. This will cause believers to appreciate the divine purpose of eternal security, which is locked within the idea of a 'Wrinkle-Free' Fabric.' It is intended to encourage every believer to be confident in their relationship with Jesus and be amazed at his wonders. Crumpled, squeezed, hidden beneath layers of life's burdens, seemingly ruined, yet in time, this fabric is automatically restored. This is Glorious! But this is merely a shadow, a type, pointing to a supreme spiritual reality. This spiritual reality is that the "Unwrinkleable Soul" of the redeemed is for Jesus, from out of a world filled with sin, to present a believer without spot, wrinkle, or blemish before the Father (Ephesians 5:27). The fabric a believer is made out of is not cheap, but a Divine Masterpiece. They are woven with unbreakable threads.

> *'For we are his workmanship, created in Christ Jesus for good works, which God prepared beforehand, that we should walk in them." (Ephesians 2:10)*

Believers should not be carried away by "discount spirituality." This is a spirituality that takes the form of godliness, but denies the power, sacrifice, and cost thereof (2 Timothy 3:5). Believers' salvation is not mass-produced, bargain spirituality. It is a "Divine Masterpiece"! The Weaver is Elohim, the Triune God! The threads are red, unbreakable threads dyed in the blood of Jesus (1 Peter 1:18-19)! This is the golden thread of eternal covenant (Hebrews 13:20); The imperishable thread of the Holy Spirit's seal (Ephesians 1:13-14); Woven into a believer who was once a "wrinkled fabric." A wrinkled fabric was man's humanity, scarred by the Fall, bearing the wrinkles of sin, folded by brokenness, crumpled in appearance by earthly struggle. But through the "mystery-patterns and exceptional designs," believers' fabrics have been restored! This is the sovereign design of God, which, through trials, becomes testimony. Weaknesses are a showcase of His strength (2 Corinthians 12:9). The scars of life are transformed into badges of glory, reflecting His multi-layered grace. The world may see wrinkles, but the Spirit sees the emerging, intricate pattern of the image and likeness of Jesus (Romans 8:29).

"He restores my soul; He leads me in the paths of righteousness for His name's sake." (Psalm 23:3)

Life's pressures for believers come in layers—accusation, disappointment, worldly stress, and spiritual warfare—piling on relentlessly. The soul may feel crushed, marred, and defeated, like garments crammed into darkness. Yet, Scripture reminds us: *"If you faint in the day of trouble, your strength is small"* (Proverbs 24:10). The enemy may label believers as irreparably damaged, but God declares otherwise. *"The LORD hear thee in the day of trouble; the name of the God of Jacob defend thee; send thee help from the sanctuary, and strengthen thee out of Zion"* (Psalm 20:1-2).

Believers are not defined by life's pressures but by God's promises. The divine fabric of their being is woven with eternal security and restorative power. Though the human spirit is

recreated at salvation (2 Corinthians 5:17; John 3:5-6), the soul is restored through the renewing of the mind in alignment with God's Word and Spirit (Romans 12:2). When the world squeezes, the recreated spirit stands firm, and restoration becomes *spiritually automatic*—not through human effort, but by the sovereign work of the Word, the Spirit, and grace.
As believers yield to God, soaking in His presence and allowing His Word to cleanse their minds, the wrinkles of despair, folds of fear, and crumples of condemnation begin to lift. In God's perfect timing, His restorative power transforms them into His masterpiece. This is the nature of the New Creation in Christ: *"Bless the Lord, O my soul, and forget not all his benefits, who forgives all your iniquity, who heals all your diseases"* (Psalm 103:2-3).

This restoration is not superficial; it is deep, holistic, and miraculous.

- **He Forgives All My Sins**: The deepest stain of guilt is removed by the blood of Jesus (1 John 1:7, 9). Restoration to righteousness is immediate, granting believers boldness to approach the throne of grace, already forgiven and cleansed (Hebrews 4:16).
- **He Heals All My Diseases**: This includes the wounds of the soul—bitterness, anxiety, unforgiveness, and brokenness. As believers yield, the Spirit applies the Healer's balm, smoothing the crumpled fabric of their lives with His healing virtue (Isaiah 53:4-5; Matthew 8:17).

The wrinkle-free nature of a believer's spirit is a testament to God's grace. Restoration isn't just beautifying—it's transformative, holistic, and miraculous.

Chapter 9

God's Tapestry of Hope: Breaking Barriers and Moving Mountains

Isaiah 45:2

"I will go before you and will level the mountains; I will break down gates of bronze and cut through bars of iron."

This is a divine promise of a God who is a "Barrier-Breaker and Way-Maker." God directly addresses Cyrus, the Persian king, and calls him his "anointed." This title was previously reserved for Israel's kings and priests. It is now applied to a pagan ruler who does not yet know God (Isaiah 45:4-5). This points to a foundational truth revealed in the life of Esther. God's sovereignty transcends religious and national boundaries, and he anoints individuals for specific purposes within his plan and purpose. The prophecy foretells how God will use Cyrus to conquer Babylon, shatter its barriers, and release his chosen people to return to Jerusalem and rebuild the temple. This act of deliverance again becomes a powerful testament to his saving power. It is strong encouragement for spiritual mobilization, alignment, and expansion. God desires to work through and in believers. Isaiah delivers this promise to Cyrus, God's anointed, before he even knew the Lord (Isaiah 45:1–4). God declared that he himself would go ahead to break barriers, dismantle locked gates, and flatten insurmountable mountains. This verse reveals a timeless principle: when God ordains a mission, he becomes the Barriers-Breaker and Way-Maker.

Mountains represent spiritual obstacles that appear

difficult to overcome, such as fear, opposition, lack, tradition, or spiritual resistance. Bronze gates and iron bars represent worldly systems, demonic strongholds, and organizational hindrances that resist spiritual and physical progress. According to God's word and examples from the examples of David and Joshua, no wall is too strong, no gate too fortified, no mountain too high for Him to break apart for His chosen ones. Notice the phrase, "I will go before you." This speaks of God's advanced presence. Breaking down barriers does not start with human effort; it begins with divine intervention. When Israel stood before the Red Sea, it was God who parted the waters (Exodus 14:21–22). When Jericho's walls stood tall, it was God's power in Israel's obedience to "shout" that brought them down (Joshua 6:20). Every spiritual barrier is first addressed in the unseen realm by God Himself before it manifests in the natural. A Spirit-filled believer does not confront barriers alone; the King of Glory marches ahead as the Breaker and Way-Maker (Micah 2:13).

Barriers are opportunities for God's glory. Barriers are not merely obstructions, but divine stages through which God reveals His glory. The mountain before Zerubbabel was not just a hindrance; it became the platform for God to declare, "Not by might nor by power, but by My Spirit" (Zechariah 4:6–7). The blind man that Jesus healed was not blind because of sin, but for the glory of God - "Neither this man nor his parents sinned," said Jesus, "but this happened so that the works of God might be displayed in him. (John 9:3). Barriers test faith, but also magnify grace. The seemingly impenetrable prison of Philippi became the platform for Paul and Silas' midnight praise and for the salvation of the jailer's household (Acts 16:25–34). For a believer, every barrier is a testimony in disguise. Jesus is the central figure and the ultimate conclusion of the Old Testament scriptures. He embodies the promise of breaking barriers and making ways out of no way. At His death on the Cross, the veil of the temple tore from the top to the bottom (Matthew 27:51), breaking the ultimate spiritual barrier, sin's separation from God. Through His resurrection, Jesus removed the iron bars of death and Hell (Revelation 1:18). Thus, Isaiah 45:2 finds ultimate fulfillment in Christ, who not only breaks barriers but makes way to transform believers into barrier-breakers and way-makers. For the Spirit-filled believer, barriers are dismantled through, Prophetic intercession – speaking the Word to mountains (Mark 11:23); Praise warfare – lifting high the sound that causes walls to collapse (2 Chronicles 20:22); Faith action – stepping into the Red Sea before it parts (Hebrews 11:29); And Unity in the Spirit – barriers fall when God's people advance as one Body (Acts 2:1–4).

A Tapestry of Defense

Psalm 91:1–4 (NKJV)

He who dwells in the secret place of the most high shall abide under the shadow of the almighty. 2) I will say of the Lord, "He is my refuge and my fortress; My God, in Him I will trust." 3) Surely he shall deliver you from the snare of the [a]fowler And from the perilous pestilence. 4) he shall cover you with His feathers, and under his wings you shall take refuge; his truth shall be your shield and buckler.

God's plan for believers is a spiritually woven tapestry where defense is not an afterthought, but woven into it as part of a believer's destiny. Breakthrough is the pattern that marks the believer's path to this destiny. In fact, a breakthrough is a key part of the believer's journey to this destiny. It is what makes the life of a believer adventurous and impactful.

Psalm 91 provides us with spiritual insight into the intricacies of living spiritually protected. It explains how a believer breaks barriers, moves mountains, and occupies territories spiritually and physically. "He who dwells in the secret place of the Most High..." "Dwells" in Hebrew is from a root word that means to sit, to remain, and to inhabit in the English language. It means being a permanent resident, not a temporary visitor. "Secret place" conveys the idea of a believer being hidden, covered, and concealed, even though a believer may be visible to the naked eye; spiritually, the believer is hidden in Jesus by the blood. It refers to a believer's spiritual dimension, not a physical location. It implies a spiritual closeness with Jesus that grants access to profound revelation and divine guidance. "Most High" denotes the highest authority, beyond every principality or power. This passage is simply letting believers know that to break barriers, a believer must dwell, not visit, in the realm of the spirit with intimacy with Jesus. The secret place is not a church building; it's a spiritual stance, attitude, and position of the heart of a believer. It also speaks to the believer's frequency of alignment with Jesus.

> *"I will say of the LORD, 'He is my refuge and my fortress; My God, in Him I will trust.'"*

"Refuge" here refers to a shelter from the deadly

storms of spiritual attacks. It is a divine place and position of fearlessness in Christ. A posture of physical and spiritual safety. "Fortress" carries the idea of a military stronghold, that is spiritually and physically fortified and impenetrable. "Trust" means to be bold, confident, and spiritually and mentally secure. This is what makes a believer bold in their declaration of breakthrough. A believer's confession of "He is my fortress" is not just a comforting statement, but a spiritual declaration. Believer's words are supernaturally powerful; they spiritually build walls, open gates, and move mountains. A believer's faith-filled confession turns protection into possession. When believers speak of God as their refuge, they are activating spiritual procedures of defense and dominion. "Surely He shall deliver you from the snare of the fowler and from the perilous pestilence." "Snare" spiritually refers to hidden traps and plans of the enemy. It symbolizes any plot of deception, delay, or spiritual sabotage. "Fowler" is anything or anyone that sets traps with evil intent. It is demonic intelligence, human conspiracies, or barriers generated by a system (Daniel 6:4-6). "Pestilence" signifies "destruction," often plagues, epidemics, or economic crises. God is not just believers' defense against visible threats, but he delivers them from hidden traps, those invisible forces that attempt to limit your destiny, derail your purpose, or delay your assignment. Example, Daniel in the lions' den (Daniel 6). The "snare of the fowler" was a political conspiracy, yet God delivered him because Daniel dwelt in the presence of God. "He shall cover you with His feathers, and under His wings you shall take refuge; His truth shall be your shield and buckler."

"Cover" here refers to wrapping around and being entangled with a screen that weaves a protective layer. "Feathers or Wings" is a symbol of God's tender yet powerful protection. It is the picture of the cherubim over the mercy seat; God's throne of grace, a spiritual defense. "Truth" is faithfulness, reliability, and divine integrity. "Shield" refers to a large body shield, something that covers a person from head to toe. "Buckler" is a smaller, supportive shield that can also serve as a weapon, used in close combat. God's truth is both armor and artillery. When internalized, it not only protects but also gives you the offensive capacity to move mountains and confront lies. God shields you from destruction, whether spiritual, emotional, or produced by a system. Dwelling in Him gives you insight, discernment, and supernatural deliverance. Isaiah 45:2 says, "I will go before you and make the crooked places straight; I will break in pieces the gates of bronze and cut the bars of iron." Faith and prophetic declaration are mountain-moving acts of believers (Mark 11:23). Psalm 91 empowers believers to speak from the secret place of God, declare from a place of safety, and command from a position of authority. Zechariah 4:7 – "Who are you, O great mountain? Before Zerubbabel, you shall become a plain!" "…Thus says the Lord: 'Tomorrow about this time a seah (about 8 gallons) of fine flour shall be sold for a shekel, and two seahs of barley for a shekel, at the gate of Samaria.' " So, an officer on whose hand the king leaned answered the man… "Look, if the Lord would make windows in heaven, could this thing be?" And he said, "In fact, you shall see it with your eyes, but you shall not eat of it" (2 Kings 7:1-2). God is not just protecting believers to survive, He's positioning believers to possess. Every promise in Psalm 91 points toward territorial authority, encompassing spiritual, geographical, and generational realms. Deuteronomy 11:24 – "Every place on which the sole of your foot treads shall be yours…" For example, Joshua, after Moses' death, was empowered by God's presence to conquer lands (Joshua 1:3–5). Psalm 91 is not just about safety; it's about spiritual strategy. It's a tapestry of defense that empowers a believer for deliverance from demonic traps, faith to move mountains, and the anointing to claim territory. When a believer dwells in the secret place, they are not hiding from battle; they are being positioned to win it.

Chapter 10

The Tapestry of The Altar

Genesis 8:20-21

"Then Noah built an altar to the Lord and, taking some of all the clean animals and clean birds, he sacrificed burnt offerings on it. The Lord smelled the pleasing aroma and said in His heart: 'Never again will I curse the ground because of humans…"

This is the beginning of the altar, a thread of covenant: man offers, God responds —a divine pattern is woven into eternity. From Genesis to Revelation, the altar is never a casual pile of stones but the divinely designated loom upon which heaven weaves its threads into the lives of men. At Noah's altar after the flood (Genesis 8:20–21), he was not merely sacrificing; he was establishing a covenant-thread with God. Every altar is a weaving point where divine promise and human obedience intersect. The altar is not a physical place as some believers sometimes imagine; it is God's weaving table. It is the loom that holds together His eternal purpose and the believers' surrender and sacrifices. Every altar carried three essential threads: blood, fire, and covenant. Blood (Leviticus 17:11) represents the red thread of atonement, foreshadowing the Lamb slain from the foundation of the world (Revelation 13:8). Fire represents the Holy Spirit's consuming and sanctifying work (Leviticus 9:24; Acts 2:3). Covenant represents the pattern of God's eternal design, woven into the lives of believers (Genesis 15; Hebrews 8:6). Together, these threads formed the divine tapestry of redemption, each altar anticipating the ultimate altar of the Cross.

The Old Testament altars pointed forward to the Cross of Jesus Christ, the final and perfect altar. Hebrews 13:10–12 tells us, "We have an altar from which those who minister at the tabernacle have no right to eat." Christ became both the altar and the sacrifice, weaving into one fabric the righteousness of God and the mercy of God. At the Cross, the vertical thread of heaven, the divine holiness, and the horizontal thread of earth, human weakness, were interwoven through the scarlet thread of Christ's blood. The Tapestry of the Altar is revealed in the Cross: the place where eternal patterns were made visible, where salvation became accessible, and where the fabric of broken humanity was mended. Paul's encouragement in Romans 12:1, is that believers should "present their bodies as a living sacrifice, holy, acceptable to God." This means every spirit-filled believer becomes a thread woven into the altar of Christ's sacrifice. No longer do believers bring lambs or bulls; they bring their lives, obedience, and worship. The altar is no longer just stone and wood; it is the community of the redeemed, knit or joined together by the Spirit (1 Peter 2:5). The Church itself becomes an altar, with each believer a living stone, bound together into a tapestry of worship and witness upon which sacrifice to God through Christ is laid and offered.

In Revelation 8:3–5, we see the heavenly altar where the prayers of the saints rise as incense. Here, the tapestry is complete. The altar of Christ is extended into eternity, and every prayer, every tear, every sacrifice of the saints is woven into the eternal pattern. The altar was not done away with after the Cross. It continues to eternity as the meeting point of God and believers. The Tapestry of the Altar is also God's masterpiece. Each time believers bow in prayer, each act of obedience, each tear of intercession, each song of worship adds a new thread in the tapestry. The Spirit is weaving you into a living altar that cannot be broken, a tapestry that continues to generations, and a fabric whose beauty will only be fully revealed in eternity.

> *"Blessed are those who dwell in Your house; they are ever praising You" (Psalm 84:4).*

Breaking and Rebuilding Altars

1 Kings 18:30

> *"Then Elijah said to all the people, 'Come near to me.' So, all the people came near to him. And he repaired the altar of the LORD that had been torn down."*

In the days of Elijah, the prophet, the altar of God in Israel lay in ruins. The LORD's altar stood in serious wreck. The hearts of the people were split between Yahweh and Baal. The hearts of the covenant people of God had drifted into compromise. They were mixing loyalty and adoration to two opposing deities. It was a mixture of devotion to Yahweh and commitment to Baal. God's people had mixed Yahweh's worship with Baal worship in the same temple and on the same altar. Spiritually, the temple was divided, and its altar was torn. This divided temple and torn altar was what the prophet was referring to. It was a picture of double-minded devotion. The divided temple and torn altar combined represented a double-minded, wavering love for two archrivals: worship of Yahweh and Baal. It was worship that appeared very spiritual on the outside but was deceitful in the heart (Jeremiah 17:9). The true altar of the LORD, that was once the focus of covenant worship, had now been broken down and neglected. When the true altar of the LORD is torn down, it reflects a people divided in their loyalty, commitment, and worship. A broken altar symbolized a people in spiritual disorder. This was not just about altar-stones; it was about altar-hearts. The broken altar revealed broken covenant, broken commitment, and misguided worship. It was a worship of compromise. Spiritual concession had given place to demonic worship and destroyed the sacred meeting place between God and His people. Spiritually, an altar is the intersection of heaven and earth, the junction of the Spirit and the flesh, the dividing line between the eternal and the temporal. It is the place of sacrifice, covenant, and communion, against the place of pleasure, comfort, and idleness. When broken, it reveals a divided heart. James 4:8 – "Purify your hearts, you double-minded." James 1:8 calls the double-minded man "unstable in all his ways." Compromise had pulled to pieces God's place of covenant, communion, and consecration in the heart. The altar represents the heart of worship. Israel was in a season of drought, not because of the land but because of the dryness in the spirit. This was not just a physical ruin; it was a spiritual symbol of compromise. Whenever the altar is broken, covenant faithfulness is split, and compromise becomes the ruling spirit. When the altar is neglected, compromise creeps in. There are five critical conditions of a torn altars that hinders pure, sacrificial, and consecrated worship: an altar of Luke-warmness (Revelation 3:16).; an altar of fear of man (Proverbs 29:25).; an altar of hidden sinful practices (Psalm 66:18).; an altar of self-dependence (Jeremiah 17:5–7).; and an altar of silence in witness (Acts 4:20).

Repairing the altar prophetically pointed to Jesus. The altar, once built with lifeless stones, is transformed in Christ into a living structure. Believers are the "living stones" (1 Peter 2:5), woven together into a spiritual temple. The twelve stones of Elijah's altar symbolized restored covenant and relationship, each stone representing unity and divine order.

Elijah's first step in calling down fire was restoration. He repaired the altar, knowing God's fire falls only on consecration, not on disorder, compromise, or neglect. Revival begins with restoration. Jesus affirmed this in Matthew 5:23–24: *"First be reconciled to your brother, and then come and offer your gift."* Worship is powerless without restored relationships and covenant alignment.

Israel's revival didn't hinge on performance but on spiritual restoration. The fire of God's presence falls only on a whole, consecrated altar. Joel 2:12–13 calls us to the same: *"Return to Me with all your heart… Rend your hearts and not your garments."* True revival starts when the gaps of compromise are mended, and unity is restored.

Spiritual repair begins in the inner altar of the heart. Elijah first called for the repair of the altar with twelve stones (twelve tribes), symbolizing the unity of the tribes and the restoration of covenant order. Fire follows repair; glory follows consecration. Matthew 5:23–24 – reconciliation comes before sacrifice. The heart must be repaired before true worship can rise. Pentecostal fire (Acts 2:3–4) fell upon a restored "altar," 120 hearts united in prayer, consecrated and waiting. Compromise is the silent builder of false altars. It often appears harmless: tolerating sin, dividing loyalties, and remaining silent in the face of truth. Yet every yielded will to sin breaks the altar of the heart. Revelation 2:20 rebukes the church at Thyatira for tolerating Jezebel's teaching, a spiritual compromise at the heart of the church. In Matthew 6:24, Jesus declared, "No one can serve two masters." To serve him and idols is to embrace spiritual-mental disorder. Compromise does not always come in the form of outright rebellion. It often appears to be divided loyalty (Matthew 6:24: "No one can serve two masters"). Tolerance of sinful practices for convenience (Revelation 2:20 – the spirit of Jezebel). Silence when truth must be spoken (Esther 4:14 – a call to courage). These are the "small cracks" that weaken the altar. Left unchecked, they destroy the pattern and function. The word "compromise" stems from the Latin word that means "to make mutual allowances." Spiritually, compromise means giving in to the devil, grounds or space that belong to Jesus.

The "Akedah" Altar in God's Tapestry

The Altar of Surrender

The word "Akedah" in Hebrew means "the binding." In Genesis 22, it refers to the binding of Isaac on the altar. The spiritual principle is that true sacrifice in covenant with God requires basically three kinds of bindings: (1) Binding the human will by the will of God (Luke 22:42). This was evident in Isaac's surrender and Abraham's obedience to a divine instruction. (2) Binding the flesh, the natural tendency to preserve spiritual interest and divine fulfilment. (3) Binding human logic, trusting God beyond intelligent reasonings for divine purposes. Isaac was the covenant child, a seed of divine promise and destiny.

Therefore, Akedah symbolizes the act of yielding entirely to God's instruction; binding human reasoning, desire, and control and bringing them under divine submission. In the Situation of Abraham, Isaac, and the Altar, Abraham represents faith, obedience, and willingness to release that which is dear and beloved at the word of God or the voice of the Holy Spirit. This test was not about cruelty but covenant trust. Every believer is called not to hold tighter to the promise but to the Promiser? Isaac represents obedience, submission, and patient surrender. He carried the wood, submitting silently to the binding process. This was the forecasting of Jesus' submission to the cross. This willingness through patience points to surrender without resistance. The Altar of Sacrifice represents the place of covenant exchange. Man offered his fall, and God provided His substitution. At the altar, the human's will is bound, and divine provision is released. The ram caught in the thicket symbolizes substitutionary atonement, fulfilled perfectly in Christ, the Lamb of God.

As I reflect on the Altar of Sacrifice, I do not see it merely as a theological construct, but as the very foundation upon which my life and ministry have been built. In my thirty-nine years of service, I have learned that the altar is not a place of loss, but the ultimate place of covenant exchange.

I remember the beginning of this journey in 1987, on the mission fields of Yekepa, Nimba County, in Liberia. As a young man, I stood at a crossroads. To step into the unknown of West African missions required me to bind my own will—my personal ambitions and my sense of security—to the horns of the altar. It was there I learned that when man offers his "fall," God provides His substitution. Just as the ram was caught in the thicket for Abraham, I found that whenever I reached the end of my own strength, Divine Provision was already waiting.

Throughout my dual career as a Senior Pastor and a Chief Operations Officer, I have often navigated the tension between human strategy and spiritual surrender. Whether managing the complex systems of the Baltimore International Academy or discipling believers in my local church, raising church leaders, workers, and ministers, shepherding pastors, serving as chairman of the Executive Council of the U.S. District, and now serving as National Overseer providing oversight to twenty churches in the U.S. District, the principle remains: Our professional rigor must always bow to the Altar's power. My MBA and my experience in organizational development have taught me how to build structures, but only the Altar of Sacrifice can breathe life into them. There have been seasons where, despite my best strategic plans, I had to stop and recognize that Christ, the Lamb of God, had already fulfilled the "substitution" I was trying to manufacture through my own effort.

My marriage to my partner, Dr. Kona-Facia Freeman-Nepay, has been the greatest earthly witness to this truth. Together, we have lived a life where our individual wills were bound together at the altar of service, allowing God to release a global impact that neither of us could have achieved alone.

As you study the Altar, do not fear the "binding" of your will. In my life, that binding has been the secret to my freedom. When you lay down your limited "production," you make room for His unlimited "Provision."

In the economy of God, divine instruction trumps personal interest: "Take your son, your only son, whom you love…" (Gen. 22:2). The altar of Akedah teaches that obedience to God's word, even when costly, always opens the way to revelation and provision, "Jehovah Jireh" (The Lord will provide or see to it). The Akedah altar is a spiritual template for believers. Each believer is called to bind their will, desires, and dreams to the altar of surrender. Romans 12:1 calls believers to be "living sacrifices." Like Isaac, all believers are invited to trust the Father's hand even when we don't understand. Like Abraham, we are called to obey swiftly, even when it costs us dearly. The church collectively is summoned to the altar of Akedah. This call is the laying down of agendas, traditions, and even "Isaacs" of ministry success or identity, so Christ can be glorified. The Church becomes prophetic when it embodies surrender and displays Christ as the true Lamb of God. Just as the altar fire consumed the substitute, the spirit now fills surrendered lives with Holy Ghost fire. What was once so binding unto death now becomes empowering unto life. The fire that demanded sacrifice now stands as the spiritual drive for mission. The Akedah altar is the binding of self-will in obedience to divine instruction, where faith releases surrender, surrender releases provision, and provision unveils Christ. For Abraham and Isaac, it was a test and a foreshadowing; for Christ, it was fulfillment; for the believer and the Church today, it is a call to daily surrender, Spirit-empowered obedience, and prophetic witness to the Lamb of God.

To understand the Akedah's altar, one has to consider this passage in its context: The Promise of God was on the Line. The prophecy and word of God were at stake. Isaac was not just Abraham's son. He was the son of promise. God promised Abraham that through His son, Isaac, his descendants would be "as numerous as the stars in the sky" (Genesis 15:5, 17:19).

For Abraham to offer up Isaac was, from a human standpoint, to sacrifice the very promise of God itself. This was a divine challenge to elevate Abraham's faith to an almost unthinkable level. It was a divine stretch of the limited faith of man. The text clearly states that God was testing Abraham (Genesis 22:1). The test was not for God to learn something He didn't know, but to demonstrate the absolute, unwavering nature of a faith and obedience that is steadfast on Him ("Now I know that you fear God..." Genesis 22:12). The Akedah's altar is the altar on which faith in God is the believer' offering on an altar before God.

The Altar of Unfiltered Faith and Naked Obedience

Genesis 22:2

"Take your son, your only son Isaac, whom you love... and offer him there as a burnt offering on one of the mountains of which I shall tell you." (Genesis 22:2)

Before the altar of the Tabernacle in the wilderness was ever built, there was an invisible altar already put together on Mount Moriah. It was not an altar built with bronze or acacia wood, but with raw obedience and costly surrender. Abraham, the father of faith, became a living pattern for worship that costs everything. It is a worship required by God that requires a believer to lay absolutely everything on this altar as a sacrifice to "Yahweh Jireh." This altar requires a total and complete trust in God's ability. As believers release what is in their hands, Heaven releases unto them what God already has in store for them. As a believer, there is a ram in the thicket (in the spirit) for you waiting to be released. Abraham was not moved by impulse; he was moved by the living Word of God, the rhema word that breaks through the barriers of the intelligence of the human mind with divine instruction. It is Spirit-initiated obedience. Isaac, carrying the wood up the hill, becomes a prophetic image of Christ bearing His own cross up the hill of Mount Calvary (John 19:17). He was a voluntary participant, without any physical or mental resistance. This echoes the words of Jesus, "No one takes my life from me, but I lay it down of my own accord" (John 10:18). This is the level of faith that God requires of each believer —a voluntary service without force or struggle. Abraham hoped against hope, believing that God could and would raise Isaac if death or anything else were to occur. Romans 4:18-22 and Hebrews 11:17-19 assure believers that Abraham believed God could raise Isaac from the dead. This is not mere hope, but Spirit-empowered faith for resurrection, a "God kind" of faith that sees beyond death.

"Yahweh Yireh" is the name of God that reveals the Holy Trinity's involvement. When Abraham named God in that place as "Jehovah Jireh," "The Lord Will Provide," he was not just commemorating an event; he was prophesying a Person, Jesus. On that very mountain, God would once again provide a ram, but this time, it would be the Lamb of God (John 1:29), His only begotten Son. The Father provides the sacrifice. The Son becomes the sacrifice. The Spirit reveals the provision and empowers the faith to receive it. "On the mount of the Lord it shall be provided." (Gen. 22:14) But more than provision, it is revelation: the altar is where heaven opens as total worship in complete surrender, ascends, and God's eternal plan touches time. "You shall make the altar of burnt offering... a place for sacrifices to be consumed by fire" (Exodus 27:1-8). When God gave Moses the blueprint of the Tabernacle, the bronze altar stood at the entrance. It was the first piece of sacred furniture one had to pass. This altar was more than a structure; it was a continuation of Mount Moriah, which was now institutionalized in the worship life of God's people. Bronze was a symbol of judgment. The holy fire was to consume what was offered. But the bronze resists the flame, symbolizing the permanence of divine mercy amidst justice. The horns on the altar were a place of refuge (1 Kings 1:50), but only for those who came with humility.

The fire on the altar never went out. It was a continual fire precept established in Leviticus 6:13. The fire was never to go out. The people were required to continually add wood and fan the fire into flames, day and night. This continuation of "fire into flames" is echoed by the Apostle Paul's admonition not just to Timothy, but to every believer, to fan their "fires into flames" (2 Timothy 1:5-7). The Pentecostal fire that now burns within believers began on Mount Moriah, spread to the Tabernacle, and then to the Upper Room. God has always kept the fire burning. The fire that once fell on offerings now falls on people, "And there appeared to them tongues as of fire resting on each one of them" (Acts 2:3). The charcoal fire of sacrifice (John 18:18), once a place of denial for Peter, became a place of restoration when Jesus cooked fish on coals (John 21:9), and finally turns into the fire of empowerment at Pentecost.

The same spirit who enabled Abraham's faith now indwells believers, enabling them to present themselves as living sacrifices (Rom. 12:1). The altar of the new covenant is the heart, and the fire no longer consumes flesh; it ignites purpose, gifts, and witness. The Fire Is the Same: At Moriah, it was a fire for testing and obedience; In the Tabernacle, it was a fire for atonement and cleansing; At Calvary, it was a fire of judgment and redemption; And at Pentecost, it was a fire of commissioning and power. What began with a father on an isolated mountain became a people gathered around a Tabernacle, climaxed with a Person on the Cross, and burst open in a group in a fiery Upper Room. The altar has always been the meeting point of God with man. The Tabernacle's altar is a prophetic pattern, a Christ-centered fulfillment, and a spirit-filled reality. Its fire still invites everyone without any disparity.

Chapter 11

The Unshakable Hope of God's Tapestry

Hebrews 6:17-19

17 Thus God, determining to show more abundantly to the heirs of promise the [a]immutability of His counsel, [b]confirmed it by an oath, 18 that by two [c]immutable things, in which it is impossible for God to lie, we might have strong consolation, who have fled for refuge to lay hold of the hope set before us.

19 This hope we have as an anchor of the soul, both sure and steadfast, and which enters the Presence behind the veil,

The Book of Hebrews mentions two unchangeable things in verse 18. These are spiritual truths intended to support a believer's hope in God, ensuring it remains unshakable. These two immutable things are: (1) His promises He has made by His spoken or revealed word, and (2) The oath He has sworn or the vow taking by Himself to confirm these promises. These two immutable things rest in the divine guarantee that God cannot lie. God being immutable means that He is unchangeable or unchanging. The point of these verses is that it is impossible for God to lie, making His promise and oath dependable and unshakable. This is the tapestry of the Weaver that believers are woven into.

A tapestry is a woven masterpiece where countless threads, seemingly scattered and disconnected, are brought together under the hand of a master weaver. In Scripture, God is often revealed as the One who weaves and fashions the destinies of the believers into Divine patterns. Job declared, "Your hands shaped me and made me" (Job 10:8). David echoed similar idea: "For You created my inmost being; You knit me together in my mother's womb" (Psalm 139:13). The apostle Paul affirms, "We are His workmanship, created in Christ Jesus for good works" (Ephesians 2:10). This image clearly reveals that each believer is a thread in the fabric of the Divine design. Fabrics may appear in different colors and fashions, but under His all-powerful loom, every fabric has a purpose. And when threads of a fabric are woven together in place, they reveal the bigger picture of His master plan. In Hebrews, it reads, "We have this hope as an anchor for the soul, firm and secure" (Hebrews 6:19). Hope is not wishful thinking; it is an unshakable expectation grounded in God's faithfulness. It holds steady because it is anchored in Christ, the risen Lord, who is both the Alpha and Omega of the divine tapestry. The world is a place of confusion, with loose ends, tangled knots, and unfinished patterns. But from heaven's perspective, the divine tapestry is complete in Christ. This means that for the believer, hope is unshakable because the end has already been woven into the beginning. "Declaring the end from the beginning, and from ancient times things not yet done" (Isaiah 46:10). Ruth the Moabitess, in (Ruth 1–4), came from widowhood and barrenness to being grafted into the lineage of the Messiah. Ruth shows how God weaves foreign, broken threads into His salvation plan. The Cross of Christ (Acts 2:23–24) seemed to the disciples as a scattered hope, but through God's plan in the tapestry, it revealed the resurrection of Jesus. What appeared to be a failing design actually became a fabric of victory. Each of these biblical figures demonstrates that unshakable hope is not the absence of trials, but the divine weaving of trials into glory.

From a spirit-filled perspective, the Holy Spirit is the

divine transport moving back and forth across the loom of God's purposes. Paul declares, "The Spirit helps us in our weakness" (Romans 8:26) and "works all things together for good" (Romans 8:28). Every prophetic word, every spiritual gift, every groaning of intercession is a thread placed by the Spirit to ensure that Christ's pattern is formed in us. The Upper Room was the Spirit's weaving the loose threads of fearful disciples into a Spirit-filled tapestry that shook the world for Jesus (Acts 2). Therefore, it is the Spirit who enables believers to live with unshakable hope, not in human strength, but in the Holy Spirit's empowerment. Paul's vision of the Body of Christ in 1 Corinthians 12 reflects this tapestry of many parts, yet one body. Individually, believers are threads, but corporately they form a radiant fabric that covers the earth with God's glory. Spiritually, this is why unity in the Spirit is non-negotiable. When threads become loose, the tapestry appears weak. But when each thread yields to the Master's wisdom, the Church becomes a sanctuary of praise. A believer becomes a spiritual garment of defense against every spirit of heaviness and evil device, displaying the manifold wisdom and power of God (Ephesians 3:10). When life looks tangled and unclear, believers must rest in the truth that God sees the other side of the tapestry. No thread in the tapestry of the Holy is a mistake. All threads were purposefully chosen; every assignment, even the painful seasons, is woven for eternal significance. The Spirit is actively weaving prophetic destiny into our lives today. Every spiritual gift, intercessory prayer, and breakthrough is a new thread strengthening the pattern of Jesus in believers. In a period of division and disorder, the Spirit is weaving believers together into a unified, radiant tapestry of revival and global harvest.

God's tapestry of the Church in the world concludes in Revelation 21:2, where the Bride, which is the perfected Church, comes down as a woven garment of glory. Every thread, every trial, every triumph will be revealed as part of the eternal pattern. Until then, the believers' unshakable hope rests in faith in the Weaver's hands. "Being confident of this very thing, that He who began a good work in you will complete it until the day of Jesus Christ" (Philippians 1:6).

God's Tapestry of Holiness

> ***Hebrews 6:15-20 / Romans 4:16-18; 15:4*** *"For everything that was written in the past was written for our instruction, so that through endurance and the encouragement of the Scriptures, we might have hope."(Romans 15:4 BSB)*
>
> *"Whatever was written beforehand is meant to instruct us in how to live. The Scriptures impart to us encouragement and inspiration so that we can live in hope and endure all things." (Romans 15:4 TPT)*

The purpose of the word here is twofold: From these two translations, the purpose of the word is revealed: (1) The "things written beforehand," is to provide: (a) instruction and (b) encouragement, resulting in hope that empowers believers to endure through life's challenges. (2) By "Empowers" and "Endures," it means a hope that gives the power and means to become, keeps looking beyond, and pursuing. Therefore, the unshakable hope expressed in Hebrews 6:15-20, Romans 4:16-18, and 15:4 reveals in detail how, through God's Word, hope profoundly impacts and shapes the believer's faith and relationship with God. It is so much so that the believer becomes spiritually tough, inspiringly anointed, impressively capable, and mentally and emotionally indestructible. The believer becomes impossible to be easily defeated or overcome spiritually, emotionally, or even physically.

Unshakable hope is rooted in God, his word, and his character. Hope in God cannot be separated from faith in God. It stems from God's unchangeable nature. - Lamentations 3:21-24. Unshakable Hope is derived from the Word of God. The BSB translation stresses the "instruction" and "encouragement" of the Scriptures. TPT emphasizes "encouragement and inspiration" from God's Word. Divine hope does not arise from human reasoning or changing circumstances. It comes directly from God's revealed truth and promises, as outlined in the Word and the Spirit. These two are firm in agreement across every generation of believers (Isaiah 40:8). Examples: "But Daniel resolved not to defile himself with the royal food and wine, and he asked the chief official for permission not to defile himself this way" - (Daniel 1:8 NIV).

Unshakable hope is A choice. Daniel and his three friends (Hananiah, Mishael, and Azariah) were among the exiles taken from Judah to Babylon. They were taken captives and chosen for special training in the king's service, which included daily provisions from the royal table (Daniel 1:5). However, Daniel made a deliberate choice to avoid consuming this food and hoped in God's provision and sustenance. Why? A spiritual reason for Daniel's choice was obedience to God's spiritual Laws. It was an Old Testament spiritual instruction. Under the Law given by Moses, certain foods were considered unclean (Leviticus 11). By partaking of the king's meal and drink,

Daniel risked violating these instructions. A prepared meal at the Babylonian court was spiritually tampered with by having been offered as a covenant meal to idols (Daniel 1:8), making it spiritually impure from Jehovah's perspective. Things spiritually tempered with are usually reserved for spiritual purposes and have spiritual implications and effects.

Believers today stand not just on new ground, but on holy ground. What seemed impossible through human strength has been woven by the invisible hand of the Master Weaver. Our story is a tapestry—threads of hardship, strands of disappointment, and knots of delay—all now forming a glorious design of promise fulfilled. Hebrews 6:18 declares: "It is impossible for God to lie, so that we who have fled to Him for refuge might have strong encouragement to hold fast to the hope set before us." Every sacrifice, every tear, every waiting season was not wasted—it was threaded in His loom. The sanctuary before us is more than brick and mortar; it is evidence that God's oath and promise stand unshakable. What He begins, He finishes. What He speaks, He performs. Where God has situated His Church is not merely land—it is refuge, testimony, and launching ground. The Holy Spirit Himself has been the Weaver, aligning threads of favor, faith, and perseverance into a tapestry of triumph.

So, believers, lift your eyes beyond the physical and behold the eternal purpose. For the same God who gave Abraham a promise and confirmed it by His oath has given believers hope as an anchor for the soul (v.19). The Master's Tapestry is not complete yet—this is only a panel in His eternal design. The next threads will be revival, harvest, and nations.

Exodus 29:42-46 (NKJV)

42 This shall be a continual burnt offering throughout your generations at the door of the tabernacle of meeting before the Lord, where I will meet you to speak with you. 43 And there I will meet with the children of Israel, and the tabernacle shall be sanctified by My glory. 44 So I will consecrate the tabernacle of meeting and the altar. I will also consecrate both Aaron and his sons to minister to Me as priests. 45 I will dwell among the children of Israel and will be their God. 46 And they shall know that I am the Lord their God, who brought them up out of the land of Egypt, that I may dwell among them. I am the Lord their God.

God empowered Moses with detailed instructions for constructing the Ark of the Covenant, the Table of Showbread, the Lampstand, and other furnishings. – (Exodus 25–31). God also declared He would meet the Israelites at the Tabernacle, which was to be "sanctified by the presence of His glory" (v. 43). By carrying out God's instructions, both Aaron and the tabernacle items were automatically spiritually consecrated for a holy purpose. Carrying out God's instructions for the Tabernacle established the holiness of the Tabernacle (Exodus 29:43–44). It was a copy of the Tabernacle in Heaven (Hebrews 9:12, 21-25). The word "Tabernacle" is derived from a Hebrew word meaning "dwelling place" or "sanctuary." It was God's visible expression of His desire to dwell among His people. "And let them make Me a sanctuary; that I may dwell among them" (Exodus 25:8). "They serve at a sanctuary that is a copy and shadow of what is in heaven" (Hebrews 8:5). The Tabernacle was a spiritual pattern that pointed to Jesus and a diagram of the believer's spiritual journey. It revealed the path of salvation, from sin to sanctification, from spiritual death to eternal life with Jesus. Each area —the Outer Court, the Holy Place, and the Most Holy Place —represented a deeper stage of relationship and revelation. This three-fold design reflected heaven's reality, the three-fold nature of God (Father, Son, Spirit), and the three-part being of man (spirit, soul, body).

In the Old Testament, the Tabernacle was not merely a tent; it was a divine revelation in fabric, wood, and gold. It was the meeting place between a holy God and redeemed people, designed by heaven but built on earth. Every thread, color, and measurement was given by divine instruction to Moses on Mount Sinai (Exodus 25–31). It was the visible manifestation of an invisible God. The Tabernacle's holiness was that items in the "Temple" were not simple designs; they were instruments with spiritual significance for divine services and encountering them was considered sacred to God (Exodus 3:5). These were items that pointed to specific aspects of the holiness of God. They were representations of God's ownership, character, and authority. Acknowledging spiritual respect for them was a way of showing respect for God's holiness and His supreme authority. Mishandling or mismanaging them was a direct offense to God's character and integrity. Every single item pointed to Jesus in His specific roles.

Under the Old Covenant, these items bore witness to God's presence. The Ark of the Covenant and Temple articles were dedicated to God and, therefore, carried God's presence. When the Ark of God containing the Covenant was brought into Solomon's Temple, the glory of the Lord filled the house such that the priests couldn't stand to minister. – (2 Chronicles 5:13–14). 1 Samuel 6:19–20 says that some men of Beth-shemesh looked into the Ark, and many died because they treated God's holy presence with casual curiosity. 2 Samuel 6:6–7, lets believers know that Uzzah, son of Aaron, also a priest of the Temple, reached out to steady the Ark as it was transported improperly. Though well-intended, it violated God's instruction (Numbers 4:15; 1 Chronicles 15:13–15). The son of Aaron, who tried to prevent the Ark from falling, died. It was to teach Israel that holiness is not to be taken lightly. The spiritual truth here is that the Ark was a sign of God's immediate presence, and it was not to be approached without spiritual preparation and divine recognition. The word "holy" meant divinely unique and set apart for specific purposes. What God set apart is spiritually unique and must never be interfered with without acknowledging divine instructions. King Belshazzar dishonored the holy vessels taken from the Jerusalem Temple by using them in a pagan feast. Immediately, a supernatural sign, the handwriting on the wall, pronounced a divine judgment. – (Daniel 5:1–5) When King Herod, standing before the people, assumed the title dedicated unto God, an angel immediately struck him with a sickness, an infestation of worms (Acts 12:20-24). Under the New Covenant, the presence of God has made its Temple in the bodies of believers, individually and collectively. In 1 Corinthians 3:16-17, the Apostle referred to the entire Church as the Temple or Body. In 1 Corinthians 6:19-20, the Apostle specifically addresses immorality as a significant spiritual offense to God's presence in a believer, who is a bearer of His Temple or Body. The spiritual truth here is that when holy objects reserved for divine purposes were treated as common, the spiritual impact was severe because of God's demand for reverence. The Lord's Supper (Communion) is an example of this disregard for Jesus' presence. In 1 Corinthians 11:27–29, Paul warns believers that participating in the Lord's Supper unworthily brings about spiritual consequences. While it doesn't determine a believer's entry into eternity with Jesus, it certainly has a spiritually negative picture of a believer's honoring of the Lord's instruction. Such an attitude also leads to their ineffectiveness in other spiritual matters dear to Jesus. He addresses it as a cause of divisions and spiritual disrespect among the Corinthians. Paul's teaching is that communion is a sacred observance set apart to remember Christ's Body as a living and sacrificial Temple. Communion is not merely a ritual; it is a spiritual act with profound consequences. A worshipful experience through spiritual preparation and examination of the heart as required.

Spiritual gifts, such as prophecy, tongues, and healing, are empowered by the Holy Spirit for the edification of the church. They are not natural talents but sanctified enablement for spiritual impact (1 Corinthians 12–14). In 2 Timothy 1:6, Paul exhorts Timothy to "fan into flame the gift of God" given through the laying on of hands. God's gifts through the Holy Spirit are spiritual deposits that must be managed faithfully. These God-given gifts are holy tools for ministry. Abusing them for personal gain or neglecting them for worldly pursuits dishonors God and affects the Body of Christ.

Maintaining Jehovah's Covenant Identity

Daniel 1:15 (NKJV)

15 And at the end of ten days their features appeared better and fatter in flesh than all the young men who ate the portion of the king's delicacies.

Throughout Scripture, "spiritually tempered" or holy things carry significant spiritual impact because God sets them apart for His divine purposes. From the Old Testament tabernacle utensils and anointing oil to the New Testament Lord's Supper and spiritual gifts, the principle holds true: what is consecrated to God must be approached with awe, worship, admiration, and respect. They are to be used according to His design and guarded against misuse. For believers today, this emphasizes that true holiness is not about outward form but about right relationship with God and obedient stewardship of the things He calls holy. Doing so leads to powerful encounters with God, a deep awareness of His presence, and a testimony that reflects the sacredness of believers' calling in Christ. Believers are not to treat sacred things, be they communion elements, spiritual gifts, or services dedicated to God, as common. Embracing a life set apart for God means we align our actions with His commands, recognizing that God's glory and power accompany what is devoted to Him. Doing so means respecting God's boundaries. From Nadab and Abihu's strange fire to Belshazzar's misuse of temple vessels, Scripture illustrates that unauthorized appropriation of what's sacred provokes divine judgment. Believers are stewards of the spiritual resources given to them by Jesus. Whether it's the Old Testament anointing or the New Testament spiritual gifts, these resources are not for self-exaltation but for God's glory and service to His people.

Things, such as spiritual obligations, practices, and services dedicated to God, are to be considered by believers as holy. Holiness heightened a spiritual Sense of God's Presence. Handling devoted things nurtures a deep awareness of God's reality. As believers honor what is to be set apart as sacred, their faith will be enriched by spiritual encounters with His presence. Daniel's ultimate aim was to exalt the God of Israel before the Babylonian officials. His decision not to eat food offered to idols and pray when he knew it would put his life in danger led to a powerful testimony of God's existence in a foreign land. The Holy Spirit functions powerfully and effectively in the lives of those who are fully submitted to Him. God is the ultimate authority over the kingdom and the rulers of the world. After the ten-day test, Daniel and his friends appeared healthier than those who ate the king's food (Daniel 1:15). God's provision and blessing displayed His glory even in areas foreign to His name and existence. Daniel's refusal was an act of loyalty to Israel's God. Rather than abandoning his spiritual heritage, he maintained it even while in captivity in a foreign land. Daniel chose to remain faithful.

Obedience to God's instructions symbolizes a believer's devotion to God's covenant. By doing so, Daniel also distinguished God's people from surrounding nations (Exodus 19:5–6). Upholding God's holiness means avoiding compromising with idolatrous practices, which include items dedicated or offered to false gods. Babylonian palace meals often involved food first dedicated to their gods. For Daniel, eating such food would be a form of participating, even indirectly, in idol worship (1 Corinthians 10:18–22). A believer's holiness means guarding God's holiness from being compromised. Daniel saw holiness not merely as an external matter, but as an issue of the heart. By refusing the king's diet, he declared that his allegiance and reverence belonged to the Lord alone, regardless of how appealing the cultural offers or pressures were (Exodus 34:14). By requesting a simpler diet of vegetables and water (Daniel 1:12), Daniel demonstrated his faith in God's provision. Daniel trusted that God would sustain and honor their commitment. This was a tangible act of faith, demonstrating that God was able to keep them healthy and strong without relying on royal luxuries. A believer's hope and faith are built through endurance. The unshakable hope is the one that has been tested and proven in real-life trials. Endurance refines a believer's hope (James 1:2–4) and strengthens a believer's faith in Christ's position with unshakable confidence in God. Throughout Scripture, "spiritually tampered" or holy things carry significant spiritual impact because God sets them apart for His divine purposes. From the Old Testament tabernacle utensils and anointing oil to the New Testament Lord's Supper and spiritual gifts, the principle holds true. What is consecrated to God must be approached with reverence, used according to His design, and guarded against misuse.

For believers today, this highlights that true holiness is not about outward form but about right relationship with God and obedient stewardship of the things He calls holy. Doing so leads to powerful encounters with God, a deep sense of His presence, and a testimony that reflects the sacredness of believers' calling in Christ. Believers must not treat sacred things, be they communion elements, spiritual gifts, or services dedicated to God, as common. Embracing a life set apart for God means we align our actions with His commands, recognizing that God's glory and power accompany what is devoted to Him. Respecting God's spiritual boundaries is critical to God's holiness and character. From Nadab and Abihu's strange fire to Belshazzar's misuse of temple vessels, Scripture illustrates that unauthorized appropriation of what's sacred provokes divine consequences. Whether it's the anointing (Old Testament) or spiritual gifts (New Testament), these resources are not for self-exaltation but for God's glory and service to His people. This is a high awareness of God's Presence. Handling holy things nurtures a deep awareness of God's reality. As believers honor what He sets apart, our faith is enriched by encounters with His presence.

Prophetic Declaration

Daniel 1:1-8-16; 3:28-30 NIV

"The chief official gave them new names: To Daniel, he gave the name Belteshazzar; to Hananiah, Shadrach; to Mishael, Meshach; and to Azariah, Abednego. But Daniel resolved not to defile himself with the royal food and wine, and he asked the chief official for permission not to defile himself this way." - (Daniel 1:7, 8 NIV)

16 Shadrach, Meshach, and Abednego replied to the king, "O Nebuchadnezzar, we have no need to answer you in this matter.
17 If the God whom we serve exists, then He is able to deliver us from the blazing fiery furnace and from your hand, O king. 18 But even if He does not, let it be known to you, O king, that we will not serve your gods or worship the golden statue you have set up." (Daniel 3:16-18).

Today, we will begin a series on divine choices through prophetic declaration. Prophetic declaration is the spiritual act of speaking spiritually of future conditions in the present situation. It is the nature of a spiritual conversion through the power of the sacred act of calling a specific aspect of life into being. The positions of Daniel and the Hebrew boys were not acts of rebellion. This was not a gross disrespect to established authority, but a matter of covenantal identification, spiritual positioning, and agreement through faith in God. It was a matter of divine choice or spiritual confession! It was a matter of establishing spiritual authority ruling over their lives (Romans 6:16):

A prophetic declaration is a spiritually inspired pronouncement through authoritative speaking. For believers, it is scripturally inspired words that carry the power to shape reality and bring about spiritual or natural change. It is by faith, declaring God's will or promises into a situation. It operates as a spiritual weapon to disrupt undesirable conditions, seal success, and call divine favor into existence. It is a believer operating from their empowered heavenly position of spiritual authority (Ephesians 2:6). These are not just ordinary words, but divinely empowered statements that carry the force of God's power. Prophetic declarations are spiritual conversations that actively engage with the spiritual realm to bring about what the Lord has already promised to believers. It is usually aligned with scriptural promises and principles. Believers are encouraged to pronounce what God has already made available in His Word.

The purpose is to cause a shift in the realm of the spirit, disrupt spiritual hostility, unlock divine favor, and transform impossible circumstances into life-changing testimonies. In scripture, prophets spoke prophetically concerning God's plan and future promises. In the New Testament teachings, it's revealed that believers are joint heirs with Jesus, exercising divine authority to make pronouncements that align with God's heavenly realm. When a prophetic declaration is made with faith, it influences and shapes circumstances. It is revealed in Scripture that prophetic declarations brought about action and national change (2 Kings 7:1). They are used as spiritual weapons to repel darkness, destroy yokes, and seal success for the believer. The purpose is to cause a shift in the realm of the spirit, disrupt spiritual hostility, unlock divine favor, and transform impossible circumstances into life-changing testimonies.

In scripture, prophets spoke prophetically concerning God's plan and future promises. Engaging in prophetic declarations is a way to trigger God's power by faith, bringing His will to pass in the natural realm. Daniel 5, from a scriptural perspective, is filled with powerful revelations of: God's holiness (that which is sacred to God and must not be defiled); Divine-ruling (consequences precede spiritual disobedience), and the forceful command of faithfulness (divine favor demands acknowledgement, discipline, and obedience). God is "Absolute!" To say "God is Absolute" is to affirm that He is the ultimate authority, above all other powers. He is self-existent, needing nothing outside Himself to exist. He is sovereign and supreme; His will is final. He is unchanging and eternal, not subject to instability or decay. He defines reality and truth. He answers to no higher law or standard. Spiritually speaking, God's "absoluteness" means that His word is ultimate. His glory cannot be diminished or challenged. His rulings are final.

In Exodus 3:14 (ESV), God declares, "I AM WHO I AM." In Isaiah 46:9–10 (ESV), He says by the Spirit, "I am

God, and there is no other; I am God, and there is none like me, declaring the end from the beginning…" These are foundational statements of God's absoluteness. He exists in and of Himself. No cause. No beginning. No end. No dependency. All these are in the situation of handling trust or covenant commitments held sacred before God. A believer cannot be aware of all of these and not take a position for Him when it is required. The Scripture says it is required that a steward be found faithful (1 Corinthians 4:2).

The Power of The Spiritual Act of Naming

Daniel 1:6-8

6 Now from among those of the sons of Judah were Daniel, Hananiah, Mishael, and Azariah. 7 To them the chief of the eunuchs gave names: he gave Daniel the name Belteshazzar; to Hananiah, Shadrach; to Mishael, Meshach; and to Azariah, Abed-Nego.

8 But Daniel purposed in his heart that he would not defile himself with the portion of the king's delicacies, nor with the wine which he drank; therefore he requested of the chief of the eunuchs that he might not defile himself.

Understanding the importance and spiritual significance of names in Scripture involves recognizing how naming is a spiritual act and has been used to: transform character, fulfill spiritual objectives or divine purposes, reinforce spiritual subjections or values of divine calling, and establish covenantal identities. It is abundantly clear throughout the Bible that names, spiritually assigned or changed, deeply affect a person's identity, role, destiny, and spiritual authority. It serves as a powerful spiritual link by which deities and spirits transfer their ideologies, intentions, purposes, and missions to individuals and communities. Differences between naturally given names and spiritually given names lie mainly in their origin, purpose, meaning, and the spiritual consequences connected to them. Notwithstanding, both acts are identity-driven and spiritually influenced, consciously or subconsciously. A name spiritually links individuals to heritage, values, and aspirations. It is a powerful spiritual act that reflects the interconnection of culture, spirituality, and individuality. (Genesis 2:11-15, 19-20). A naturally given name is a generated idea. It is a name influenced, chosen, or generated by human parents or family members at birth. It serves primarily a cultural, family, and natural identification purpose. Usually, it reflects family heritage, culture, circumstances around birth, personal preferences, or ancestral lineage. Nevertheless, it holds significance spiritually, culturally, and emotionally, but may not necessarily represent divine purpose or prophetic destiny; it still has a behavioral impact. It is mainly linked to natural conditions and identity, which may have spiritual causes. The name "Abram" meant "Exalted Father." It was a cultural name with spiritual intentions given by Terah, his biological father, suggesting a natural hope for future leadership within the immediate family. The name Abraham, which means "Father of a Multitude, was given by God. This name change reflects God's divine purpose to use Abraham as His illustration of faith and as a family head, not just of his immediate family, but of nations and people. It was a spiritual shift from a personal identity to a larger divine purpose. (Genesis 17:1-8).

Jacob's name, naturally given by his parents (Isaac and Rebekah), means "heel grabber," "supplanter," or "one who follows closely behind," literally describing circumstances at birth, reflecting his early life of deception. (Genesis 25:25-26). Israel means "He Struggles with God" or "Prince of God." The change happened after Jacob wrestled with "The Angel or Spirit of God" and prevailed at Peniel (Genesis 32:24-30). It marked Jacob's transition from a man who relied on cunning to one who relied on God. His new name reflected a transformed character and a new identity as the father of the 12 tribes of Israel. A Spiritually-given name is divinely or spirit-generated. A spiritually-generated name is higher in spiritual influence than mere cultural or family importance. It embodies prophetic destiny, spiritual authority, divine purpose, and transformation of identity. It is a spiritually given name assigned or changed directly by a spirit's intervention or through divine inspiration. It usually signifies divine purpose, destiny, spiritual calling, or a change in spiritual status or relationship. A name divinely or spiritually revealed is often made known through dreams, visions, prophetic utterances, or angelic visitations (Luke 1:31; Matthew 1:21). It embodies spiritual purpose, calling, destiny, and identity when given from Heaven as ordained by God. It has spiritual authority, blessing, divine empowerment, and prophetic significance. It is also an indication of a spiritual shift in a person's life, often marking a covenant-tie or a deep spiritual connection with God or other spiritual bodies. Repeatedly calling a name associated with a foreign or strange spirit or god carries significant spiritual implications and consequences. It invokes spiritual presence. Equally so, when God changes a person's name, as He did with Abram to Abraham, repeatedly calling it brought the prophecy to pass. A name holds deep spiritual meaning and real-life impact. To conform and convert these young Jews, they had to be broken physically and culturally, mentally, and spiritually. This was an elusive spiritual attack through convergence and conversion. It had to be a spiritual attack intended for these young Jews to be "grafted and embedded" into the Babylonian culture, traditions, and worship. Therefore, the ruler of spirits ruling over Babylon attempted several things to be done to them: First, their names were to be spiritually changed (Daniel 1:7) to the names of the gods and the spirit of Babylon. Second, they had to be adopted into Babylonian culture through food, clothing, and behavior. Third, they had to be converted to the spiritual or worship practices of the strange spirits of Babylon.

There are essential differences between the two major sources of a name change. A change of name by God is life-giving, purposeful, and aligned with His divine plan. A name received from a strange power or spirit is often followed by oppressive spirits seeking to manipulate, control, misrepresent, or destroy God-given identity and divinely intended destiny. A God-given name brings blessing, authority, and divine arrangements of God's purposes in the life of a believer. A name from a strange spirit can lead to spiritual bondage, confusion, and estrangement from God. A God-given name can lead to spiritual fulfillment, a lasting legacy, and spiritual growth. A name from a strange spirit or god comes with the demand for the offering of strange fire (Leviticus 10:1-2). Offering strange fire hinders true spiritual progress, stunts growth, and creates barriers to God's purposes. A strange fire is an unauthorized, demonic, and profane sacrifice and worship offered on God's altar. For a Spirit-filled believer, the spiritual importance of a name depends on its source. When God gives a name, it is a powerful act of deliverance, identity, and purpose, as seen in Abraham's life. However, being called by a name tied to a spirit other than the Spirit of God can lead to spiritual depression and confusion. It is a weakening of one's connection to God. The most important thing for believers is to remain rooted in their God-given identity and resist any attempt by the enemy to distort or destroy it. This is what the Hebrew boys chose to do.

***

Daniel 1:6-8

God's first commission to Adam was to give him the authority to name the creation (Genesis 2:19-20). This was not merely an administrative act; it was an act of demonstrating the authority of dominion delegated to him. When Adam named each creature, he perceived its nature—this was not intellectual categorization but spiritual interpretation. What he named, it became. The spoken word sets identity. Similarly, in creation, God said, and it came to be (Genesis 1). Thus, naming is a creative act that echoes divine speech. This shows that naming is integrally linked to authority and dominion (Psalm 8:6-8). The Babylonian attack was, therefore, an attempt to seize this created order. The Tapestry of God is woven in divine identity and destiny. Divine identity and destiny are woven through the intentional threads of spiritual naming. In the Tapestry framework, every thread represents divine design, function, and purpose. Naming integrates the person or believer into the spiritual loom of God, who gives pattern and meaning to each believer or thread in His Tapestry.

Naming is the thread of divine identity operating as the mark of God's hand on a person or a believer's life. In the Tapestry of God, every believer is a unique thread woven by the Creator's design (Ephesians 2:10). A name that is from the Lord operates like the color or pattern that identifies a thread assigned by the Divine Weaver. When God renamed Abram to Abraham and Jacob to Israel, He was not only rebranding; He was also reweaving a new life. He was removing their old identities and weaving new ones into their lives and futures. A new identity according to His divine intention. Thus, naming is not cosmetic; it is constructive, it shapes the thread's spiritual DNA (Isaiah 62:2-3).

In God's tapestry, believers find their divine connections. Each time God names or renames, He defines the texture and function of that thread in the larger pattern of His redemptive plan. In God's tapestry, believers are threads of transformation from the natural to spiritual pattern. Each believer is a thread in the Divine Tapestry, a distinct color, texture, and design woven by God's intention. A God-given name carries divine imprint and prophetic DNA. When God changes a name, He redefines the function and future of that thread (Revelation 2:17). The weaving of a new tapestry usually starts with the use of raw materials, including natural fibers that are dyed, stretched, and refined before being woven. Likewise, a name generated naturally represents a raw or natural human beginning. When the Spirit of God steps into the life of a person, He assigns them a new identity, which signifies spiritual processing and divine transformation. Divine transformation is not patches of fabric put together to form a new one. It is a total transformation from an old fabric to a completely new one. This is a spiritual fabric.

Every part of this fabric is spiritually brand new. It is like the transformation of a caterpillar into a butterfly. Example: Abram ("exalted father") becomes Abraham ("father of nations"), a transition from limited expectation to limitless covenant.

God rewove Abraham's thread with a broader prophetic description. The change of name represented a shift in the weaving pattern from family promise to generational destiny. The loom of God is the vertical thread of God that provides the believer's thread with the spiritual backbone of resistance against the enemy's temptations and deceptions. The intent of the spirit of Babylon in this world today is to reweave every soul in the pattern and directions of evil and demonic spirits through false worship (2 Corinthians 11:13-15). The devil's tapestry is a carbon copy of God's tapestry in appearance, but woven in a reverse pattern with an identity and destiny marked by no future and no hope.

In Daniel 1, Babylon sought to rename the Hebrew youths to align them with false spiritual threads, attempting to reprogram their divine pattern into a Babylonian one. This was not cultural convenience; it was an attempt to spiritually take over their lives and annex them to the Babylonians' culture and worship. It was an effort to cut them from the Tapestry of God and graft them into the tapestry of idols. Daniel and his companions, the three Hebrew boys, Hananiah, Mishael, and Azariah, refused to let their divine thread be rewoven into a strange fabric. Their faith in Yahweh was the spiritual resistance that preserved the purity of God's Tapestry in their lives. In spiritual terms, to accept a false name is to accept a false thread. In the modern believer's life, refusing ungodly identity labels (fear, failure, addiction, compromise) is an act of remaining woven into God's holy design. Naming is a divine weaving of relationship in Christ. It is the thread of a covenant with Jesus. In the Bible, naming usually ushers a person into alignment with God's covenant. When God names, He claims ownership (Isaiah 43:1); when the world names, it claims control. Divine naming weaves a person into a covenant with Jesus, marking them as His workmanship. Example: Simon became Peter ("rock"), marking him as foundational to the Church's establishment (Matthew 16:18).

In the Tapestry of God, covenant names are woven with threads of permanence and purpose, reflecting both the authority and stability of divine craftsmanship. Renaming in Christ is a thread of restoration, redeeming broken patterns in the lives of believers. Just as God restored Jacob's broken identity into Israel's destiny, He continues to restore slanted threads within the Tapestry of His people. The enemy often names a person after their past failures or current suffering, keeping them in bondage through the name. God names or renames them in Christ, bringing them into their purpose and future. The Hebrew names given to the three boys elevated and empowered them spiritually. The Babylonian names given to them held them in bondage to the gods of Babylon.

Divine renaming is the restoration of pattern, aligning the believer back to the original divine design before corruption or cultural infiltration. It is God reweaving what the enemy tried to unthread. In the Tapestry of God, the act of naming is the act of weaving. Each time God calls a name, He pulls a thread into alignment. Each time the enemy renames, he attempts to tangle it. Every divine renaming in Scripture symbolizes restoration of divine order. The enemy intends to rename by shame; God wants to rename by grace (Ruth 1:20-21; 4:14-17). The spiritual act of naming determines which pattern a life will belong to: Babylon's confusion or Zion's beauty. This act calls believers to a response of choice. It brought to the minds of the Hebrew boys a profound awareness of the spiritual significance of their identity in Christ. This awareness empowered them to resist the "Babylonian" naming patterns of this age. Naming is a crucial and timely thread in the beautiful, complex, and redemptive tapestry of God's plan for believers.

Economic Righteousness

Daniel 5:1-31

From a Spirit-filled, biblically grounded standpoint, Economic-Righteousness can be defined as: "The just, holy, and accountable management of wealth-power and financial-influence under God's sovereign rule, reflecting reverence for His holiness and righteousness in both private and public life."

In Daniel 5, we witness two striking scenes: (1) The direct contrast between unrighteous and righteous economics, not merely in terms of money, but in how resources, authority, and sacred trust confided to a steward can be considered and handled. (2) The spiritual and prophetic revelation of the Aramaic term "Mene, Mene, Tekel, and Parsin," flooded with deep spiritual truth and warning. From a spiritual perspective, Daniel 5 is packed with powerful revelations of God's holiness, divine ruling, and the extreme importance of faithfulness, particularly in the context of handling sacred trust or covenant commitments before God. King Belshazzar, ruler of Babylon (possibly a son or descendant of Nebuchadnezzar), held a spiritually disrespectful feast in which he: "…gave orders to bring in the gold and silver goblets that Nebuchadnezzar, his father, had taken from the temple in Jerusalem, so that (he) the king and his nobles, his wives and his concubines might drink from them" (Daniel 5:2, NIV).

These were vessels (2 Corinthians 4:7) dedicated unto God for holy service in the "Temple of Yahweh." Belshazzar decided to use them in a profane act of celebration, combining sacred elements of Jehovah with pagan worship, praising "gods of gold and silver" (v. 4). It was then that a mysterious hand appears, writing a mysterious message on the wall near the "lampstand" (Daniel 5:5). This same "finger of God" that wrote the divine-ruling in Babylon is now working through the Holy Spirit to bring freedom, healing, and the Kingdom of God to believers today (Luke 11:20). Daniel made it clear in verse 24: "Therefore, He sent the hand that wrote the inscription." This "hand" was a messenger of God's ruling, a symbol of divine authority and spiritual intervention. It signifies that God is not distant as some would like to believe, even in the pagan courts of Babylon. He always makes His presence obvious and felt, especially when it concerns His holiness. Throughout Scripture, Jehovah at times manifested His presence directly, without the mediation of a human vessel, to reveal His sovereignty, holiness, and supremacy over all other powers. These manifestations are often called "manifestations of divine self-revelation" (1 Samuel 5:1-5; Acts 12:21-23; Exodus 19:16-20). In all these accounts, God's direct manifestations reveal a pattern; His presence is not confined to vessels, but vessels exist to steward His presence. When He acts without them, He reminds creation that He alone is God. His sovereignty extends to every nation, ruler, and people. This reflects the majestic rule of God. His kingdom is over all kingdoms. The "hand" wasn't God Himself but sent on a divine assignment just as God sends angels, prophets, and even judgments. The holy vessels represented God's treasures, valuables, and prized possessions. This was why God's anger was stirred. The misuse of the Temple vessels is spiritually serious, and His action can be heavy. These vessels were put in the Temple at the direction of God to Moses (Exodus 25:8-9). They were spiritually purposeful unto God and represented His authority. Therefore, these vessels were sanctified, set apart for the use of esteeming worship, and holiness unto the Lord. To use what is holy for profane purposes, especially to glorify idols, is an act of spiritual treason. Belshazzar violated sacred boundaries, bringing truth and error into an unholy alliance.

This mirrors modern-day spiritual disrespect in the face of God. This is where many blend truths with error, Spirit with flesh, and holy purposes with carnal ambition. Spiritual disrespect in the face of God occurs when believers mix holiness with worldliness, compromising the sovereignty of God (like Belshazzar using holy vessels for drunken idolatry). Just as vessels can be misused, so can the gifts of the Holy Spirit, financial resources, and sacred callings. When God's sacred things, things consecrated and dedicated to His services for covenant use, are manipulated for entertainment, profit, or ego, the fear of the Lord departs, sacred or covenant trust is broken, and divine ruling is inevitable. God does not deny such a person entry into eternity, but He does give such a person over to a "reprobate mind." A reprobate mind is a spiritually corrupt mind that repeatedly refuses to submit to the words of Jesus, the will of God, and the leading of the Holy Spirit. To be given over to such a mind is for the Holy Spirit to turn a believer over to the carnal mind for spiritual guidance and direction.

In this passage, the monetary terms reflect the idea of value and accountability. In a spiritual context, misuse of sacred or covenant finances, such as tithes and offerings, is a modern equivalent to what Belshazzar did. Examples: Using "dedicated" funds for personal luxury; Manipulating offerings through false promises; preaching prosperity without integrity or holiness. The church, collectively, is now the temple (1 Cor. 3:16), and we are living vessels. Misusing what should be considered dedicated resources is a serious offense before God. Acts 5 (Ananias and Sapphira) is a clear New Testament example. They lied to the Holy Spirit about an offering and fell dead, not because they kept the money, but because they made up excuses and lied about what was devoted to God. Babylon is symbolic of confusion, mixture, and rebellion throughout Scripture (Revelation 17–18). The key offense of Babylon is mixing holy things with profane (Malachi 3:1-4, 6, 13-18; Haggai 1:5-9). Blending worship of Yahweh with idols. In this way, modern "Babylon" can be: compromised churches; celebrity Christianity; Doctrines that minimize holiness and exalt man. Belshazzar represents this spirit of careless arrogance, and Daniel stands as a model of faithfulness, discernment, and separation.

Daniel 5:1–31

Daniel 5 is not merely an ancient account of Babylon's fall; It is the scripture's account of a divine audit, an economic-righteousness inspection conducted by the Holy Spirit Himself.

"Mene, Mene, Tekel, Upharsin" was not just a mysterious writing; it was Heaven's audit report. It was delivered to a king of a kingdom that had mismanaged both God's sacred trust and the stewardship of influence He temporarily permitted. The seizing of Jerusalem was not the triumph of an ungodly empire over God, but rather a disciplinary measure arranged by Jehovah to awaken a spiritually insensitive people. What appeared as defeat was, in truth, divine redirection. God handed His covenant people into Babylonian captivity not for destruction, but for revelation, to reintroduce Himself as the one true God amid nations that had crowned idols.

"...so that the living may know that the Most High rules in the kingdom of men and gives it to whomever He wills..." (Daniel 4:17). When Nebuchadnezzar captured the vessels of the temple (Daniel 1:1–2), he unknowingly became a custodian of sacred things. Though Babylon took Jerusalem, Jehovah had taken Babylon's king as a temporary steward. The vessels, the people, and even the wisdom of the captive Jews became instruments through which God's holiness and dominion would be revealed. "The king's heart is in the hand of the Lord; like the rivers of water, He turns it wherever He wishes" (Proverbs 21:1).

Therefore, Nebuchadnezzar, Darius, and even Cyrus were not self-appointed rulers; they were divinely recruited stewards, chosen for a season to manage what eventually belonged to God. Through them, God audited the nations and revealed His glory in distant courts of law. The phrase "Mene, Mene, Tekel, Upharsin" points out four layers of divine economic and honest evaluation:

Mene - Numbered: God measures every economy, every ruler, every ministry. Divine resources, time, and trust are never without accountability. Tekel - Weighed: Heaven weighs motives, integrity, and stewardship. Financial prosperity without spiritual commitment to holiness tips the scales against righteousness. Peres (Parsin) - Divided: Whatever that is considered holy unto God, when mismanaged, is divided; what is holy but profaned is reassigned to another vessel of faithfulness. Belshazzar inherited Babylon's throne but not Nebuchadnezzar's humility. His failure was not in having gold, but in desecrating the sacred, turning holy vessels into instruments of vanity. He mixed righteousness with fleshly entertainment, covenant symbols with carnal pleasure. This is the essence of spiritual economic perversion, when sacred resources, time, gifts, finances, and position or influence are spent on gratifying the self rather than on divine purpose. "You have been weighed on the scales and found wanting" (Daniel 5:27). In modern terms, God is auditing the Church today for the same reason. When consecrated vessels (believers, ministries, or finances) are used for self-glory rather than divine glory, Heaven releases an audit notice. From a Spirit-filled perspective, Daniel 5 shows the Holy Spirit's pattern of intervention when stewardship fails. The hand that wrote on the wall was not God Himself, but a divinely commissioned manifestation, a manifestation of divine self-revelation. Throughout Scripture, God has used such visible interventions to reaffirm His holiness and justice. The collapse of Dagon before the Ark (1 Samuel 5:1–5), the death of Herod (Acts 12:21–23), and the shaking of Sinai (Exodus 19:16–20). In each, God bypassed human mediators to announce, "I alone am God."

The same is true in the situation in the palace of Babylon. God disrupted the pride of man with supernatural handwriting, indicating that when the world's systems reach a peak of spiritual and ethical disregard, the Lord intervenes directly or indirectly to restore the order and purpose of God. "For the Lord is the Judge; He brings one down and exalts another" (Psalm 75:7). Divene audit is to spiritually evaluate accuracy, truthfulness, and integrity against Heaven's standard. Spiritually, God's Word and His Spirit are the measuring scales. The Spirit-filled believer lives under continual audit, not of condemnation, but of alignment. When the Church allows the Spirit to weigh its motives, the handwriting on our walls becomes words of affirmation, not judgment. Economic righteousness, therefore, is not about the abundance of resources a believer has but the alignment of those resources with divine purpose. The faithful steward says, "Is this God's intention?" The carnal steward says, "What's in it for me?" Heaven's audit seeks those who can handle abundance without greed and arrogance, and manage influence without idolatry.

"If then you have not been faithful in the unrighteous mammon, who will commit to your trust the true riches?" (Luke 16:11). Just as God used Nebuchadnezzar and Darius as temporary stewards to manifest His sovereignty, today He is raising Spirit-filled Daniels, men and women who will govern faithfully in Babylon without becoming Babylonian. They understand that economic righteousness is not a doctrine of prosperity but a discipline of accountability. They discern that holiness is Heaven's currency and stewardship is the economy of the Kingdom. In a time when many misuse the vessels of God, manipulating offerings, monetizing the sacred gifts and offices, and profaning worship, God is again writing on the walls of ministries, markets, and nations. The same Spirit who once wrote judgment now writes

restoration on hearts willing to repent and realign. "The silver is Mine and the gold is Mine, says the Lord of Hosts" (Haggai 2:8). A divine audit is not intended by God to end with despair, but with a revelation of divine truth. While the King was physically dethroned, Daniel and the Hebrew boys remained spiritually enthroned in Babylon, a land that was anti-Jehovah. Righteous stewardship will always outlast worldly stewardship. When God weighs His people spiritually, He does so not to condemn but to correct and restore, not to humiliate but to highlight faithfulness. Every divine audit is an act of love, a spiritual call to restore and elevate sacred trust. The handwriting on a believer's wall is never final; Jehovah's grace always is. "For judgment must begin at the house of God" (1 Peter 4:17).

Here lies God's unshakable hope of divine choice. God still chooses faithful stewards to reveal His glory among the nations. In this generation, God is raising Daniels with apostolic integrity and prophetic wisdom, men and women who will pass Heaven's audit. Their hearts will not tremble before the handwriting of judgment, for their stewardship is anchored in righteousness. They will carry a holy audit trail, every coin accounted for, every gift sanctified, every influence surrendered, until the kingdoms of this world become the Kingdom of our God and of His Christ. "And the government shall be upon His shoulder…" (Isaiah 9:6). In the Tapestry of God, every thread represents a divine entrustment, life, calling, resources, and purpose. When God allows a believer to go through the world's captivity, He is not discarding His design but rethreading the pattern of their destiny. Babylon became the loom, and Nebuchadnezzar, Darius, and Cyrus were temporary weaving tools in God's hand. God used them to redefine and realign the threads of Israel's destiny until their colors and purpose aligned once again with His divine pattern. "The Lord has made everything for its purpose, even the wicked for the day of trouble" (Proverbs 16:4). "He changes times and seasons; He removes kings and sets up kings" (Daniel 2:21).

Key Themes and References

1. **The Divine Tapestry and Workmanship (Ephesians 2:10; Spiritual Formation)**

   Ephesians 2:10 Commentary and Exegesis:

   - O'Brien, P. T. (1999). The Letter to the Ephesians (The Pillar New Testament Commentary). Eerdmans.
     Best, E. (1998). Ephesians (International Critical Commentary). T&T Clark.

   The Tapestry Metaphor in Spiritual Life:

   - Corrie ten Boom's "Tapestry" Analogy:
   - Willard, Dallas. (2002). Renovation of the Heart:

2. **Hope as the Anchor of the Soul (Hebrews 6:19)**

   Hebrews Commentary on Anchor and Hope:

   - Lane, W. L. (1991). Hebrews 9–13 (Word Biblical Commentary).
     Thomas Nelson.
   - Attridge, H. W. (1989). The Epistle to the Hebrews (Hermeneia). Fortress Press.

3. **Grace and Corporate Unity (1 Corinthians 15:10; Ephesians 4:1-6; 1 Peter 2:9)**

   Corporate Tapestry / Body of Christ:

   - Barth, M. (1974). Ephesians: Translation and

Commentary on Chapters 4–6 (Anchor Bible). Doubleday.

- Fee, G. D. (2014). The First Epistle to the Corinthians (Revised Edition, New International Commentary on the New Testament). Eerdmans.

Royal Priesthood and Chosen People (1 Peter 2:9):

- Jobes, K. H. (2005). 1 Peter (Baker Exegetical Commentary on the New Testament). Baker Academic.

4. **Joseph's Life as a Prophetic Pattern (Genesis 50:20; Romans 8:28)**

Typological Interpretation of Joseph

- Sarna, N. M. (1989). Genesis (The JPS Torah Commentary). Jewish Publication Society.
- Chrysostom, John. Homilies on Genesis.
- Moo, D. J. (1996). The Epistle to the Romans (New International Commentary on the New Testament). Eerdmans.

ACKNOWLEDGEMENTS

To the Almighty God the Master Weaver whose sovereign hand threads every moment, every revelation, and every assignment into His divine tapestry. This book exists because of His grace, His word, and His unfailing guidance.

To my spiritual covering, **Bishop Dr. Darlingston G. Johnson**, Presiding Prelate of Harvest Intercontinental Ministries Unlimited, my mentor, spiritual father, and apostolic voice. Your teaching, guidance, and example have shaped my theology, ministry, and understanding of spiritual purpose.

To **Bishop S. Musa Korfeh, Diocesan Bishop**, whose invitation to minister at his 10th Bishopric Anniversary created the sacred moment in which the Lord birthed the revelation that later became *The Tapestry of God*. Your leadership, honor, and apostolic generosity have blessed my life and ministry.

To the leaders and members of **Harvest Intercontinental Church–Baltimore**, thank you for your steadfast support, your encouragement, and your hunger for the Word. Your receptivity to teaching and your loyalty to the vision continually strengthen my hands for the work of ministry.

A special word of appreciation to the **5:00 AM Prayer Team**, whose daily devotion, intercession, and expectation have served as a constant source of inspiration. Your faithfulness to prayer and your engagement with the daily devotions helped give this work rhythm and momentum. Thank you for standing in the gap and for pressing into God with such consistency and passion.

To my editorial team, whose excellence elevated this manuscript into its final form:

Mrs. Wayétu Moore, Principal Editor, acclaimed, best selling author whose work has been featured in *The New York Times*, and Winner of the Inge Feltrinelli Prize for Nonfiction. Thank you for lending your literary brilliance, editorial precision, and creative insight to this project. Your stewardship of the manuscript strengthened its voice and sharpened its impact.

Minister Benjamin Freeman, Compiler, Editorial Liaison, and Associate Editor. Thank you for serving as the bridge between author and editor, for your meticulous compilation work, and for your devotion to ensuring the manuscript's clarity and coherence. Your own gifts as an author, recognized in Monticello, Virginia, enrich everything you touch.

Exhorter Daykaker "DK" Karter, Technical Advisor, Media Director, and Publicist. Thank you for your expertise, meticulousness, and dedication to presenting this work with excellence. Your media leadership at Harvest Intercontinental Church–Baltimore continues to be a blessing.

To every intercessor, friend, and ministry partner who prayed, encouraged, or supported this assignment your contributions, seen and unseen, are deeply appreciated.

To my beloved wife, **Dr. Kona Facia Freeman Nepay**, whose wisdom, strength, and unfailing support undergird every dimension of my calling. Thank you for believing in this work, for walking beside me with grace, and for personifying the beauty of partnership in ministry.

Finally, to every reader may the Lord use this book to awaken purpose, mobilize destiny, and align your life with His divine design. May you discover your place inside the tapestry God is weaving across the earth.

About the Author

Apostle Patrick K. Nepay is a visionary leader, seasoned administrator, and devoted minister with more than **37 years of unwavering service to the Gospel of Jesus Christ**. His ministry journey began in 1987 on the mission field in Yekepa, Nimba County, Liberia, an experience that shaped his global outlook on faith, community transformation, and Kingdom advancement.

Ecclesiastical Leadership

Apostle Nepay is the **Founder and Senior Pastor** of Harvest Intercontinental Church–Baltimore, where he has spent decades cultivating a vibrant, missiondriven congregation rooted in prayer, discipleship, and global evangelism. His influence extends nationally as the **National Overseer of the U.S.District of Harvest Intercontinental Ministries Unlimited (HIM-U)**. In this role, he provides apostolic oversight, strategic leadership, and spiritual covering to **twenty churches** across the region. His ministry is marked by integrity, compassion, and a steadfast commitment to raising leaders who impact generations.

Professional & Educational Excellence

Beyond the pulpit, Apostle Nepay is a **highly skilled strategist** with more than **20 years of expertise** in school operations, production management, and organizational development. He is the **CoFounder and Chief Operations Officer** of Baltimore International Academy Inc. (BIA), a multilingual immersion and International Baccalaureate World School. Since the organization's founding in 2006 and the school's opening in 2007, he has been instrumental in building the systems, facilities, and operational efficiencies that sustain the institution's continued success.

His professional accomplishments are supported by a strong academic foundation:

- **MBA**, (with distinction) University of Wales Trinity St. David
- **B.A. in Biblical Studies**, Carolina University
- **Certified Public Manager (CPM)**, University of Baltimore

Personal Life

At the center of Apostle Nepay's life and ministry is his family. He is joyfully married to his partner in purpose, **Dr. KonaFacia FreemanNepay**. Their enduring union rooted in faith, education, and service stands as a testament to shared vision and unwavering commitment to uplifting others. Together, they continue to build, lead, and inspire with grace, excellence, and devotion to the Kingdom of God.